Silent Agreements

Advance Praise for

SILENT AGREEMENTS

"The insightful authors of *Silent Agreements* offer clarity on how we can approach and resolve those challenging unspoken issues between ourselves and others without fear. They will help illuminate new pathways of understanding, and foster open communication in all your relationships. I recommend this very helpful book for anyone who is committed to creating happy, healthy relationships."

—Katherine Woodward Thomas, *New York Times*
bestselling author of *Conscious Uncoupling*

"What a cogent, insightful look at how the agreements we think are presumed and assumed by the very people we most want to understand us rarely are, because of what never gets said. This wise book gives profound voice to the inner silences that can trip up all of our relationships, be they with loved ones or workplace partners. A must-read for those wanting to be truly heard."

—Audrey Edwards, coauthor of *Children of the
Dream: The Psychology of Black Success*

"We live in an age of ambiguity, in which miscommunication and insincerity are epidemic. This is a time in which people are quick to judge and just as quick to condemn. *Silent Agreements* is a useful reminder that unexamined certainty is almost always a mistake. But it is first and foremost a book about clarity and how to obtain it. In this age when we are desperately attempting to clarify rules governing consent, where many remain confused over whether yes means yes or no means no, *Silent Agreements* is hugely illuminating. It is a timely and valued contribution to our mutual understanding not only of each other but of our collective selves. For navigating the often-unspoken assumptions that govern relationships between family members, friends, lovers, spouses, and coworkers, it is the perfect guide."

—Ellis Cose, author of *The Rage of a Privileged Class* and *The End of Anger*

"Silent agreements: what a provocative idea! The authors clearly describe the kinds of silent agreements that can be problematic at home, work, and play, and provide helpful and easy-to-implement advice about how to identify and overcome these powerful expectations that may otherwise derail our relationships."

—Matt Bloom, associate professor at the University of Notre Dame

Silent Agreements

How to Free
Your Relationships of
Unspoken Expectations

Linda D. Anderson, Ph.D.
Sonia R. Banks, Ph.D.
Michele L. Owens, Ph.D.

RODALE.
NEW YORK

Copyright © 2019 by Sessions Innovations in Psychology LLC

All rights reserved.
Published in the United States by Rodale Books, an imprint of the
Crown Publishing Group, a division of Penguin Random House
LLC, New York.
crownpublishing.com
rodalebooks.com

RODALE and the Plant colophon are registered trademarks of
Penguin Random House LLC.

SILENT AGREEMENTS is a registered trademark of Sessions
Innovations in Psychology LLC.

Library of Congress Cataloging-in-Publication Data
Names: Anderson, Linda D., author. | Banks, Sonia R., author. |
    Owens, Michele L., author.
Title: Silent agreements / Linda Anderson, Ph.D., Sonia Banks,
    Ph.D., Michele Owens, Ph.D.
Description: First edition. | New York : Rodale Books, [2019]
Identifiers: LCCN 2018046999 | ISBN 9781635653465 (pbk. : alk.
    paper) | ISBN 9781984822918 (ebook)
Subjects: LCSH: Expectation (Psychology) | Interpersonal
    relations—Psychological aspects. | Interpersonal conflict.
Classification: LCC BF323.E8 A54 2019 | DDC 158.1—dc23
    LC record available at https://lccn.loc.gov/2018046999

ISBN 978-1-63565-346-5
Ebook ISBN 978-1-9848-2291-8

PRINTED IN THE UNITED STATES OF AMERICA

Cover design by Sarah Horgan

10 9 8 7 6 5 4 3 2 1
First Edition

This book is dedicated to our parents, extended family of relatives, close friends, colleagues, and clients for supporting, challenging, and believing in us all along the way. They learned to love silent agreements as much as we do.

To Calvin Reid, Jr., our chief inspirer, for believing in us and providing unwavering support from the very beginning of our journey

MICHELE
Bill and Marcus, who bring the sunshine, and with whom my silent agreement is simply to love

LINDA
Saleem, my spiritual and life partner, as well as Jordan and Naren, my beloved home team with whom I share great pride and joy

SONIA
Olivia and John, who teach and model the power of opening silent agreements every day

Between what is said and not meant, and what is meant and not said, most of love is lost.

Kahlil Gibran

CONTENTS

Silent Agreements

WHAT SILENT AGREEMENTS ARE AND HOW THEY AFFECT OUR RELATIONSHIPS

Romantic relationships often begin like the opening scene of a romantic comedy. Two people meet, and oh my God! We like the same music! We *both* want to try hang gliding? Wait, you're allergic to cats, *too*? It's about attraction, connection, and yes, hormones. In the beginning, everybody is as attractive and charming as a movie star. Then reality creeps in and the warm, delicious glow begins to fade. Turns out he's really not into holding doors open for you and doesn't like live music. And surprise! She hates tennis and doesn't agree with everything you say. So now what?

Or how about when you start a new job? You begin with the highest expectations. You're going to work hard and introduce fantastic ideas to the company. You're going to go above and beyond. And in no time, they'll charge into your office with offers of a big raise, right? Then you realize that your boss has a temper, and you spend much of your time trying to placate him. He also promotes his favorite people while overlooking the best employees. You do your best to be a team player, but what you really want are greater challenges, a bigger office, and more money. You wonder, "How did I get *into* this spot, and how do I get out of it?" In both of these scenarios, silent agreements are at play.

WHAT ARE SILENT AGREEMENTS?

Silent agreements are the unspoken "rules" of your relationships. They grow from the assumptions, expectations, and beliefs that you don't talk about but still hold others accountable for. They appear in every kind of relationship, and as you read on, you'll probably discover that you're participating in several silent agreements. Some may have been in place for a very long time. Your earliest relationships have great influence on many of your behaviors, decisions, and both conscious and unconscious motives, so in these pages you're going to learn about how your childhood experiences have also influenced your part in silent agreements.

Silent agreements sound something like this: "His mother is allowed to criticize my cooking, but I'm not supposed to respond." "The boss doesn't offer me a raise, and he knows I won't ask for one." "My daughter is getting good grades, so I stay out of her schoolwork." Such agreements can continue indefinitely, often without discussion, because of fear, guilt, feelings of obligation, or aversion to conflict. Sometimes they continue because they're healthy and they work, but more often than not, they hinder rather than help your relationships.

Because you don't share your agreements aloud, complications in your relationships can arise. You may believe that the other person understands the terms of the silent agreement and is in full alignment with you on it. Consider how many times you've said something like "He should know that already" or "Why would I have to tell her that?" You may perceive an unspoken issue one way while the other person may have an entirely different view of it.

When you have silent agreements with others, you proceed as if all parties agree about what is expected in the relationship, about who fulfills which expectations and how they're "supposed to" do so. Sometimes your beliefs, expectations, and assumptions are well matched, and even though you never talk about them, the silent agreement and your relationship hold hands and merrily march along. But more often, such expectations don't line up at all. Sometimes both parties are aware of the other's expectations but aren't ready to address them. If you keep them silent, they pave the way for misunderstanding, disappointment, and relationship drama because you evaluate and react to your relationships based on how well or poorly the other person cooperates with the mismatched silent agreement. Often you try to avoid talking about a silent agreement because you feel that you have too much to lose if you bring the issue to the surface. In these circumstances, your fear of damaging the relationship keeps you quiet. You may not even be aware of your silent agreements or of the unspoken beliefs and expectations that feed them. In this case, you have unconsciously agreed to something with another person without being fully aware of it.

Where do these beliefs and expectations originate? Quite often with you yourself: "I will never settle for less than my dream man." "I will sacrifice everything for my children." "My career comes first." These internal silent agreements can inform how you enter your relationships and what you expect from other people. They can also dictate the kinds of silent agreements you expect others to enter to support your silent agreements with yourself. More important, they often provide a map for how you navigate the roads of your lives—the decisions you make, the jobs you accept or reject, the friendships you form, and the family you create.

Your relationship with yourself is constrained when you don't recognize the expectations, assumptions, and beliefs you have about who you are, what's important to you, and why. When you're unaware of your beliefs about yourself, the silent agreements you enter into with others will be more difficult to uncover. Without this awareness, you assume that the other person has read and agreed to adhere to the same relationship rulebook that you have. That's when you can find yourself questioning the behavior of the other person. You find yourself wondering, "What the heck was he thinking?" when you'd be better off asking yourself, "What was *I* thinking?"

Suppose, for example, you've just chosen a new apartment to share with two of your friends, and you're deciding who is going to pay for what. Your designated bedroom, which includes a working fireplace and has a great view, is the biggest of the three. Your roommates think that you should pay more rent than they do. You disagree. This leads to heated arguments and almost breaks up your group. Then one of the friends asks you, "What is it that you find unfair about paying a little more money for more space and a fireplace? I'm guessing that you see the fairness but don't want to lose the argument." This pushes a button because it's true. You do see their point, so why won't you give in? Could it be that a long-standing silent agreement you've had with yourself ("No one is ever going to take advantage of me") is complicating the negotiations? If you haven't yet acknowledged that this agreement exists, you'll experience more moments like this one throughout your life. You can mistake them for simple differences of opinion, but with a little excavation, you'll discover how the silent agreements you have with yourself show up in your interactions with others.

A look at some psychological theories may help to clarify how silent agreements manifest themselves. Your early experiences are reinforced and layered upon as you grow and mature. For many of us, this begins with a developing sense of our parents that affects the way we see and interact with the world. If at the earliest stages of your life, your parents respond to you in a loving way and reflect back to you affirmation, approval, and acceptance, you'll view yourself as worthy and intrinsically valuable. You're likely to later manifest this in a healthy sense of self and positive interactions with others. If, on the other hand, you internalize harshness, disapproval, disengagement, or rejection, you're likely to develop a more negative sense of yourself as well as anxiety about what to expect from others. Often what you internalize is a contradictory combination of behaviors from the important people in your lives. For example, a person might be both loving and overly critical of you. This contrast complicates your ability to organize your sense of who you are and what you expect of others. You might grow to believe that you're loved but not truly accepted.

Some psychologists have posed the notion that when your view of yourself isn't reinforced through approval and responsiveness from your early caregivers, you can develop a "false self" in hopes of receiving more self-affirming responses.[1] In part, changes in behavior happen relatively normally as children are socialized and begin to shape their behavior into acceptable norms of interaction. However, in its more extreme forms, this kind of development can mean that the individuals are cut off from essential aspects of themselves and can walk through life not being who they truly are.

Why are these theories of particular interest when learning about silent agreements? Silent agreements occur in those places within yourself where you hold your true wishes, beliefs, and expectations, along with those expectations you've internalized from others. Sometimes they're formed out of a need to continue presenting the false self that you began to develop early in your life. This can happen when you're led to believe that your true self isn't appropriate or doesn't have value. For example, suppose your silent agreement with yourself is that you will never let your independence be compromised. This agreement might actually reflect the *opposite* of what your true self longs for: dependence on someone who truly loves you. But if your earliest experiences made you feel that your dependence on others would be rejected or disapproved of, you may have developed an insistence on absolute independence to protect you from experiencing disappointment and rejection by someone you truly desire to depend on.

When two people bring internalized remnants of different early experiences to their adult relationships, you can imagine the opportunities for misaligned notions about how to interact with each other and interpret each other's behavior. These remnants help to form your silent agreements with yourself, which become parts of your silent agreements with others, thus perpetuating the impact of your experiences and interactions that occurred during your early development.

Also worth considering are theories that suggest you may be susceptible to a family pattern of relating that is passed on through multiple generations. This "multigenerational transmission process"[2] can affect your ability to develop a separate sense of self but can also guide how you interact with others. Sometimes a parent veers from the traditional family patterns and conveys to their offspring (both directly and indirectly) other options for relating, emotional expression, and responsiveness. If you absorb these variations, you can develop a more separate sense of self that allows for more autonomy from these patterns. You in turn can pass on these differences to your children, and so on. Of course, family members may experience varying degrees of adherence to family precedents over generations, with some people sticking to them more than others and passing on the patterns with little variation.

For example, suppose your family passes down the notion that people should remain married no matter what. Then after generations of family members obeying this rule, your niece Kendra, who was raised by a free-spirited mother, gets divorced. Several members of the family react with disapproval, even anger. They begin to treat Kendra as an outcast. At the same time, Kendra feels relief now that she's acted with courage and in the interest of her own needs. Seeing her mother make individual choices when Kendra was growing up helped her to consider her needs separately from those of her family and to do what she believes is best for herself. This is an example of the long-standing influence of generations of the family's traditional feelings and approach toward marriage, as well as one individual's ability to distinguish herself from it. Your parents aren't the only influencers; you, your siblings, and your parents may be affected by a multigenerational family system that has been in place for a very long time, which means that supporting silent agreements might tag along for the ride. However, when family members differentiate themselves, silent agreements are often shattered, sometimes leading to family conflict and strife.

Depending on which stage of life you're currently in,[3] some silent agreements may have more meaning for you. For instance, in your twenties and thirties, you're making impactful choices about your education, occupation, friendships, and partners. Your silent agreements may be full of expectations about how your life *should* progress, whom you *should* partner with, and how that partner and others close to you *should* behave. However, at a later stage such as midlife, your needs, wishes, and expectations may have changed. By then you may have had experiences that change what you expect of yourself and of others, making it more likely that your old silent agreements will no longer serve you. In fact, your silent agreements may get in the way of new goals for your life, causing you to take stock of your old agreements and change them. In this instance, you might feel an emotional discomfort that you don't fully understand or consciously examine, but it nudges you to want to make changes in your life.

Silent agreements can have less hold later in life. You may have encountered older relatives who are very free with their opinions, who like to speak their mind, launching unvarnished comments into family conversations. Sometimes this is because they're in a stage of life during which they feel less concerned than ever with others' expectations of them, both the silent and the articulated. Freed from their own silent agreements, they're able to speak more candidly without censoring themselves out of fear.

The various theories about how and why people function as they do have informed our understanding of what silent agreements are, how they originate, and how they manifest themselves in our lives. Keep these ideas in mind, and they'll help you understand the roots and the impact of your own silent agreements.

As you move through the book, you'll read how to navigate productive "clear the air" conversations that can lead to healthier relationship choices. The tools provided will help you if you've ever:

- Stopped trying to work something out because you just didn't want to go there again.

- Kept passing up opportunities for a higher-profile job.

- Noticed recurring problems across all of your relationships.

- Been betrayed by someone you thought you really knew.

- Experienced growing distance between you and a close friend.

- Thought that issues between you and your siblings were insurmountable.

- Avoided confrontation no matter how much it cost you.

- Stayed in a troubled relationship to avoid being alone.

- Masked the real you to gain a promotion.

- Married someone because you didn't want to break their heart.

- Said yes to your kids when you knew you should have said no.

If you're like most people, these issues (and so many more) are the kinds of landmine topics that you ignore or avoid talking about to prevent conflict. Very few of us look forward to conflict, but avoiding conflict doesn't usually lead to peace. In some cases, such avoidance can even be damaging. When you remain silent out of fear, you're only delaying the inevitable. It's like ignoring a small fire; caught early, it can be put out easily, but if you refuse to take notice of it for long enough, you're going to need an entire fire department. Worse yet, in each of your relationships you've probably allowed multiple silent agreements to go unchecked, which can result in a brush fire. And when the conflict you're avoiding is a conflict within yourself, that fire will spread.

As we explore some of the ways in which silent agreements can show up in your life, you may see yourself in the stories. You'll see how pivotal experiences in your childhood, internalized messages from family and others, and the challenges you face throughout your adult development contribute to the silent agreements you create. The stories and exercises in the following chapters will help you recognize your silent agreements with yourself and those you have with others. Along the way, you'll find strategies for addressing and, if you choose, revising them.

CHAPTER 1

WHERE DO SILENT AGREEMENTS COME FROM?

For those of you who like to understand how things can get started from an individual's perspective, we offer a step-by-step progression of how silent agreements form. Here is one person's story of how it all began. As you consider Sarah's introduction to silent agreements, you might see yourself in some of these scenarios. Her story will show you how silent agreements start, grow stronger, and show up repeatedly throughout your life. Once you know where they come from, you'll be in a better position to choose a new path.

THE BEGINNING: SARAH'S SILENT AGREEMENT WITH HERSELF

Imagine that you are a young girl named Sarah. You're four years old and your family's next-door neighbor, Diane, knocks on the door, hoping to come in to schmooze with your mother, who's busy doing chores. Your mother peeks through the door, sees Diane, and mutters under her breath, "Damn. Why today? I have too much work to do." Nevertheless, she answers the door, smiling and welcoming Diane into the house. When Diane says hi to you, you tell her, "You should go home. Mommy said that she doesn't have time for yakking."

Your mother looks mortified and yells at you to not say such things. She apologizes profusely to Diane, telling her that you've been acting up all morning. She then tells you that for being such a rude girl you must sit in the corner until she tells you you can come out. You're confused and begin to cry. You try to cling to your mother, but she leads you to a chair in the corner, where you sit and cry quietly and where your mother makes clear that you'll remain until you apologize to Diane.

POWERFUL CHILDHOOD MEMORIES

This experience was a very powerful one for you. If you had never seen another example of this kind of dishonesty, the memory of the incident might have faded and have had little impact on your ideas about truth and openness. Instead, through your childhood and teen years you saw your mother modeling the same kind of behavior. She would complain and sometimes even cry about feeling burdened. But when she was face-to-face with those who generated these emotions, you'd watch her transform into an acquiescent lady who swallowed her feelings and went along with what was asked. Maybe she thought it was impolite, unpleasant, uncomfortable, or insensitive to let others know when she felt overwrought or when, for whatever reason, she just wanted to be left alone. But her actions taught you that being honest is often a poor choice when face-to-face with acquaintances, relatives, and close friends.

Within these recurring incidents are the seeds of your approach to relationships and the formation of silent agreements with yourself and others. You'll have a difficult time rejecting others for fear that doing so will lead to your being rejected and shamed yourself. You learned from your mother that when you don't want the company of another person, you shouldn't be honest about that. In the name of courtesy, she modeled dishonesty and then punished you for revealing the truth. This left you with a searing sense of shame. And you felt abandoned by the mother you thought you were helping.

What's the big lesson you learned? That telling people how you *really* feel is bad. Beyond that, and perhaps more important, you learned that your genuine feelings aren't important if someone wants something of you that you really don't want to provide.

When you witnessed these scenes during your teen years, you stood up to your mother's lack of authenticity. Sometimes you'd even berate her, but she rejected your criticism. Instead, she would explain that even when she was tired, busy, or at odds with others, she still didn't see the need to refuse people and make them feel rejected or unwanted. She explained that people didn't mean any harm but sometimes just needed her help or were too nice for her to turn away. The ramifications of this kind of "politeness" can be tremendous. For example, as a result of this thinking, your mother spent fifteen years in a relationship with a man who was clearly not a fit for her. With great frustration you watched her fight against her desire to leave him, with justifications like "He really is a nice guy." And you vowed that you'd never be a doormat or subjugate yourself to another in the interest of meeting their needs while neglecting your own. But you couldn't have known then how difficult it would be for you to stay true to that promise.

FROM FEELINGS TO SILENT AGREEMENTS: THE SARAH IN ALL OF US

Sarah's scenarios are the kinds of early experiences that teach us to enter silent agreements with ourselves and with others. It goes something like this: When you're a baby, you tend to express genuine feelings and reactions to the world around you, and as you grow, your repertoire of expressions expands. As an infant or a toddler, you might throw a toy down when you're bored with it or smack away the hand of the adult who's keeping something you want out of reach, but you eventually learn to use words to express what you're feeling. Along the way, your parents, families, and countless people you encounter out in the world teach you to express yourself in socially acceptable ways.

In this case, little Sarah was scolded for letting the neighbor know that Mom really didn't want her around. Her mother wanted to make clear that her daughter's bluntness was not going to be rewarded, and then Sarah witnessed the conflicting follow-up: Her mother was annoyed but invited the neighbor in anyway. Sarah learned that you might want someone to leave you alone, but you shouldn't *tell* them so, and her mother never advised otherwise. Sarah also learned that if you're honest in such situations, someone is going to end up embarrassed (at her age, it probably felt more like pure shame) and maybe even angry. She also learned that the other person in the situation—in this case, the neighbor—may be in on it. After all, Diane heard Sarah say that her mother wanted her to go home, but she stayed anyway. Blaming Sarah helped everyone sweep the whole thing under the rug. But the lesson was there. Put simply, Sarah learned not to express her feelings if such expression comes with any risk of causing upset.

So what happens next? We typically shut up and shove the feelings down. Sometimes we know they are there and we consciously choose not to share them. Sometimes we've shoved them down so far and for so long that either we don't know what we feel or we can't clearly determine if our feelings are still present.

One big problem with this suppression is that even feelings that seem buried will emerge through behavior. Because we carry with us doubt and fear about whether to share our feelings, we make compromises with ourselves in the form of silent agreements. We now believe that such feelings will cause difficulties if we express them aloud, so we make a deal with ourselves and with others to make life easier by staying silent.

FEEL IT, BUT DON'T REVEAL IT!

But how can a deal that you make with yourself alone be considered an agreement? In agreements with the self, it's as if there are two parts of you involved. To spare yourself other people's anger, disapproval, or rejection, or to simply spare yourself the awkwardness of confrontation, you separate the side of you that holds your genuine feelings, thoughts, and reactions and keeps the truth quiet from the side that expresses them openly. Like Sarah, whose feelings used to be nicely aligned with her willingness to express them freely but who learned to divide herself into two personas, you may feel pressed to separate these sides of yourself. So in order for you to have both feelings you'd like to express and the desire to keep the feelings secret, you have to develop a system that lets you have the feelings but keeps them concealed. That mechanism is a silent agreement.

SILENT AGREEMENTS IN YOUR RELATIONSHIPS

Silent agreements in your relationships function similarly to this but with more layers. Here you're sometimes silent about what's going on beneath the surface even though your behavior reveals you. For example, your partner experiences your genuine feelings when you act out your fear of sexual intimacy in the form of bedtime headaches. But he agrees (silently) not to say anything about it because of his fear that if you two deal with the issue openly, the real reasons for your lack of interest might be so serious that he might never be able to have sex with you again. He also wants to avoid an uncomfortable conversation about sex because he doesn't want to reveal aloud that he has no sexual confidence and therefore finds women intimidating. So he's counting on you to continue helping him keep his concerns and feelings silent, too.

LIKE MOTHER, LIKE DAUGHTER: PERPETUATING SILENT AGREEMENTS FROM THE TEEN YEARS TO ADULTHOOD

Let's revisit Sarah as a teenager. As she grows up, her relationships with men unfortunately follow the same path as her mother's, despite her vow to the contrary. After several months of dating her first high school boyfriend, Sarah decides she wants the freedom to date other boys, but her boyfriend is a genuinely nice guy whose feelings she's sensitive to, so she finds it very difficult to break up with him. Instead of just telling her boyfriend how she feels, she instead becomes increasingly irritated with him for minor things. Sarah is repeating the same silent response that she learned from her mother. Her boyfriend is shy and is afraid that he won't be able to find a girlfriend as special as Sarah, so he won't speak up and end the relationship either. They break up eventually, but only after hurtful weeks of mixed signals, drama, and spotty communication—thanks to their complementary silent agreements.

At twenty-one, a vibrant, daring young woman with dreams and ambitions, Sarah goes through the same cycle again. She meets John, an honest, straightforward small-town guy whom she views as a safe choice. She silently agrees to stay with him so she can experience her first grown-up relationship without too much challenge or risk. John, despite knowing that the two are incompatible, stays with Sarah because he craves the change and excitement that he doesn't have the nerve to create on his own. Yearning for more, she tires of the relationship. Following her past behavior, she is afraid to tell him how she feels because she fears he will become angry and reject her. Eventually the relationship comes to a contentious end.

Because Sarah does not have the tools to recognize and address her own silent agreement, as well as her silent agreements with others, this unproductive cycle continues well into adulthood. She eventually finds herself in a relationship with Dean, another good man from whom she is very different. There's not much bringing them together, but he is the first man to validate her opinions and her right to make choices based on her needs, so she marries him. For a while, his acceptance makes it easier for her to put up with their incompatibilities.

After a few years, Sarah admits this relationship isn't making her happy. To quell the anxiety about rejecting someone again, she convinces herself that she's too picky and silently remains unhappy in her marriage. Fifteen years later, Sarah is finally confident and self-aware enough to realize that staying in her marriage is intolerable and breaks her silent agreement—if she speaks her truth, it leads to anger, hurt, and rejection, just as it did when she was four. She asks Dean for a divorce.

WHY DOES SARAH CONTINUE THIS PATTERN?

Sarah's pattern of remaining in relationships for too long is a remnant of the harsh rejection and hurt she experienced when she said out loud what her mother wouldn't. This was a significant event in the early development of her anxiety about telling the truth about her feelings. As an even younger child, Sarah could sense much from her mother's body language, affect, and actions at moments when her mother struggled with her wish to be open with others but decided to stay silent instead. As is also often the case with young children, Sarah's ability to sense this occurred even before she was old enough to articulate it.

Later on, rather than acknowledge her real feelings and leave after sighting the first (or second or third) red flag, Sarah learned to act out her relationship unhappiness by nitpicking and displaying irritation and impatience, all the while hoping her partner would end the relationship so she wouldn't have to do it herself. Eventually the relationships ended because her behavior forced her feelings into the light. Only then was the silent agreement broken.

SILENT AGREEMENTS: WHAT IT ALL BOILS DOWN TO

A silent agreement between two people often reveals that both parties have thoughts and feelings that haven't been fully shared with each other, for fear of ending the relationship or having to acknowledge some untouched deep emotions. As a result of your silence, your behavior and the thoughts, feelings, and beliefs that accompany it are often misread. You've internalized this way of doing things because of the many times in your life when your open expression of feelings felt risky or received a response that made you feel anxious, ashamed, guilty, or insecure. And so you learned to create silent agreements.

How Can We Recognize Our Own Silent Agreements?

You may have silent agreements in your life when

- You're getting along on the surface, and that's where you stay—on the surface.

- What you're *not* saying has become louder to you than your ability to articulate it.

- You believe that if the truth comes out, there will be hell to pay.

- You believe it would be more painful to share what you feel than to deny it.

- Your relationship is built on knowing what *not* to bring up.

- You believe that if you talk about it, you'll lose something, or more important, someone.

You might find as well that you're in a silent agreement when you're talking about anything except what's actually bothering you. Often when you feel helpless to change a situation, you try to ignore how much it disturbs you and instead invest energy in trying to minimize or deny your feelings. At such times we tell ourselves that it's more peaceful to remain silent. And sometimes we are so unaware that even when we're talking about things, the harmful silent agreement goes on and on.

BASIC CHARACTERISTICS OF SILENT AGREEMENTS

Fear

Some silent agreements are driven by our fear that lifting the silence will allow others to truly know us. Why don't we have the courage to express our real feelings to the people we love? Why can't we speak up about our ambitions at work? Why do we continue to play the role of the little sister or brother despite the fact that we hate being treated like a child? The answers are fairly simple: We're afraid that people will hurt us, stop loving us, and maybe even leave us. We might also be afraid to admit what we really want, because what if we don't ever get it? But staying silent about your desires and needs doesn't make them go away. It just decreases the likelihood that you'll ever get what you really want.

Diversion

When you have an issue you don't want to face, you may try to find a way to hide it from others and even from yourself. In such scenarios, you do whatever it takes to divert attention from the issue and keep it underground. By their very nature, silent agreements keep your issues buried.

For example, to distract yourself from the fact that you and your mate have grown apart, you might become overly involved in your children's lives. Your mate might silently agree to participate so he can distract himself from his fear that you no longer love him. So clearly the silent agreement isn't about the kids; rather, it's a construct to let you both ignore what you fear in your relationship. Diversions like this one allow you to pretend that the diversion (in this case, the kids) is the thing in your life that needs your attention, while the real issue is moved to the background.

Multilayering

Silent agreements are usually connected to multiple beliefs, feelings, and expectations. Trying to handle all the layers of a silent agreement at once can be scary and difficult. As a result, you may choose to deal with only the top layer. When you feel that you can deal with only part of a silent agreement, you tend to address that part exclusively while denying or backing off from the rest of it.

For instance, you might believe that your husband is having an affair, but you both act as if he's just hanging out with friends, and you hope that sooner or later he'll tire of the other person. The problem here is that the real silent agreement revolves around the fact that your man has been seen hanging out in gay bars. But you can't face the idea that the "other woman" might actually be another man. That's the second layer to the silence that the two of you are keeping. He cheats with men, and because you aren't ready to accept that, you acknowledge the cheating, but not with whom he's really cheating. Your husband struggles with his behavior and can't bear what you're likely to say and do if you find out that he's gay. So he participates in this silent agreement by saying that he's just been "out with his friends." The two of you would rather silently agree to pretend that he's covering up his hookups with other women because the fact that he's having sex with men is just too complex to deal with. And if you lift that silence, you're likely to expose other deep issues that will likely cause massive upheaval.

It can be difficult to uncover all the layers of your silent agreements because one or both of you can become overwhelmed and unclear about what hurts and to what degree. In releasing the silence all at once, you may be fearful of exposing issues that will erode your entire relationship. Still, once the basic truths of your feelings and beliefs are revealed, they can provide you with a stronger foundation for a truly authentic relationship.

Change and Transformation

Silent agreements are fluid. Just as relationships go through stages, silent agreements change as well. For example, in your family, you might play the role of the compliant little sis in contrast to your bossy big sister. Both of you may be okay with these roles at first; your sister gets to feed her ego and be in control, and you get to feel protected and safe.

Later in life, you begin to explore other sides of yourself and discover that you have a gift for business. You're assertive and decisive, and your new catering business thrives. The silent agreement between you and your sister changes to accommodate your new role. Your sister becomes the proud sibling of a successful businesswoman, bragging about you to all her friends. It's a little embarrassing, but you silently agree to let her do it because you feel appreciated and you really like this new dynamic between the two of you. Through the following years, you travel extensively together, sharing unique (and expensive!) experiences, silently agreeing not to think about who's contributed what. At this point, the agreement has shifted again—you feel like equals now and fully enjoy each other's company.

Silent agreements with yourself can transform in another way. Sometimes you might avoid acknowledging the feelings you have that contradict the beliefs of your family and community. Yet despite your internal rejection of these ingrained beliefs, your behavior might reveal that you're still attached to them. This behavior can *transform* how you present yourself; you might actually end up living an alternate version of your true self. The good news is that you can learn to notice, understand, and uncover your silent agreements, face your fears, and speak your true feelings out loud. And that's a transformation that lays the foundation for an authentic life.

CHAPTER 2

THE FOUR ELEMENTS OF CHANGE

We've discussed the origins of your internal silent agreements with yourself. Now let's consider whether you and your mate, boss, relatives, or friends are bumping up against mismatched silent agreements or are on course for agreements that blend well. In this chapter, we provide a plan for silent agreement checkups in your relationships. These steps or phases can lead to truly life-changing results if you commit to exploring each one. Keep in mind that you don't need to remake the other person in order to transform the relationship. You can simply begin recognizing the conditions and restrictions your own silent agreements place on you.

This approach involves four elements or stages that will allow you to identify your silent agreements and discover what lies beneath them. This may include underlying fears and desires. These elements offer a framework for beginning the process. We believe that all four will need to be addressed, but the order in which you approach them

may vary. You may have the values in place to begin working on your silent agreements, but please recognize that
before you start, the language you use to talk to your silent
agreement partner needs to change. Below are the four
stages you'll need to go through—the four elements you'll
have to address—in changing your silent agreements.

Stage 1. Using Basic Values of Empathy, Trust, and Respect

Trust and respect are at the core of every healthy relationship, no matter how different we are from each other.
If you approach this process with a regard for the other
person as well as confidence in and reliance on his or
her goodwill, that's a great start. Recognizing that you
are each a part of the work that needs to be done and are
equally empowered will create the mutuality that allows
this process to go forward effectively. You're coming to
work things out, so make a covenant to bring your best self
to the task. Once you realize the value of mutuality in your
relationships, you'll be more equipped to identify where
you and those you care about are going wrong with one
another, and then you'll be more open to working things
out together without judgment and blame. This awareness
will help you to relax and find what you're seeking in your
relationships.

HOW TO DO IT

- Find a mutually agreeable time in a private
  environment without distractions.

- When you're addressing a workplace silent agreement, keep your conversations confidential.

- Avoid office gossip, which can sabotage your ability to find and sustain mutually agreeable solutions.

- When exploring intimate silent agreements, the tendency can be to want to talk about it with other people. To protect the process and show the greatest possible respect, do your best to keep the discussion between you and the other person involved.

While these approaches may seem obvious, sometimes in haste or an anxious need to address what's going on, people often don't adhere to them. But in order for your efforts to be truly effective, begin by laying the groundwork for the best possible communication. This means that you'll need to assert your needs, wishes, and expectations and be open to those of the other party. Nagging or insisting that the other person see it your way (otherwise known as trying to prove yourself right) should not be on this menu.

Example—Family Silent Agreement
After relocating to your city to look for a new job, your brother-in-law has moved into your home "temporarily." Six months later, he has no job and shows no signs of trying to find one or move out. Your spouse says nothing about it, but you've had it. You want your home and privacy back, and you expect your husband to tell his brother it's

time to go. Your husband doesn't want to ask his brother to leave until he has a solid opportunity in sight, but he admits that his brother has been there longer than expected.

One night you come home tired and wanting to relax, only to find your brother-in-law stretched in front of the television with snacks, a beer, and his latest love interest. You are furious with him but even more furious with your husband for not, in your mind, choosing you over his brother. It's time for a serious conversation, and it is important to conduct it so that you and your husband hear each other.

In-law issues are sensitive and potentially damaging in relationships if not handled carefully. So rather than call your husband into another room where you explode, argue, and issue an ultimatum, instead suggest a time when you and your spouse might talk about the situation. You might ask him to take a walk after dinner, join you for a drive, or have a cup of coffee at the local diner.

You're both likely to be able to talk more calmly away from the scene of the crime. Also, out of the house you won't have to censor the conversation.

WHY DO IT THIS WAY?

Setting a time will give both of you the chance to become mentally and emotionally prepared to identify and share your silent agreements. You'll probably be more focused if you aren't likely to explode in the heat of the moment. Remember that you'll be trying to uncover silent agreements that affect not only this situation but also other aspects of your relationship. It's fine to let on that you're frustrated and angry, but before the conversation begins, set the stage for free communication.

CONVERSATION STARTERS

You'll want to use language that indicates that the two of you need to work things out *together*. Even if the silent agreement you have is essentially one with yourself, you can see how others are affected by it and can become party to it. Here are some examples of how you might communicate your concerns:

- You and I share a problem. We've both let this linger. I hope we can work through this together.

- Know how much I love, trust, respect, and care about you and don't want us to act as if our problem doesn't exist.

- I need a weekend away, a time-out to get myself together so I can focus on how we can talk through this without guilt or blame.

- I'm concerned that there are issues we haven't talked about that are affecting how we solve this problem together. I wonder if you have concerns about this, too.

- Talking about this is difficult for me, but we're family and I'm hoping we can help each other say what we need to say.

Stage 2. Using Your Personal History and Insight

Here you work on understanding how former interactions with family, community, and others have shaped your feelings about yourself and spawned the secrets underlying your silent agreements. In this stage:

- You can discard any old rules, admonishments, or hand-me-down beliefs that no longer apply or work for you.

- Don't let other people "rent space" in your head. The choices you make should be your own. Try to connect what you discover about your past with how you're responding in the present.

- Use this new information to help you communicate aloud about your silent agreements.

HOW TO DO IT

Example—Family Silent Agreement
Let's look again at your struggle with the unwanted house-guest. The two of you will want to examine underlying beliefs and experiences that may be affecting your reactions. To make this easier, we've developed a helpful approach (see chapter 9). It involves a series of questions and statements to complete that will help you to uncover old ideas and rules that are now getting in the way of your relationships. For instance, as the wife in this case, you may find during this exercise that childhood hurts about feeling

displaced by visiting relatives have intensified your reaction to your brother-in-law's extended stay. Your husband does the exercise as well and perhaps realizes that his role as "the responsible one" among his siblings has clouded his judgment about knowing when to say, "Enough is enough."

WHY DO IT THIS WAY?

When you can see the situation from your partner's point of view and factor the impact of his or her past into the current equation, you'll be more likely to deal with each other in a more enlightened, empathic, and supportive way. You'll feel like more of a team.

Stage 3. Reframing—Creating a New Agreement That Works

In this stage, you're ready to consider revising your silent agreement. Consider the silent agreement that's causing the relationship the most discomfort. To reframe it, you'll need to identify the hidden issues that helped the agreement to come to be.

HOW TO DO IT

Example—Family Silent Agreement
Imagine that after doing our exercises and uncovering your past beliefs, assumptions, and expectations, you and your spouse are now able to have the following dialogue:

YOU:

> I've **always believed** that one's **spouse and children
> should have priority** over others. **I needed** this to be
> the case in our relationship because **I never felt** it was
> the case when I was growing up. When we agreed to
> let your brother live here, **I assumed** that he would
> look for a job and move out well before the year had
> passed **and assumed** you expected the same. When he
> didn't, **I expected** you as my husband and his brother
> to ask him to move. **I've been quiet while waiting** for
> you to act because **I've been afraid** that your family
> will always be more important to you than the kids
> and me.

HIM:

> I was **raised to believe** that family is the most
> important thing, too, and that **I'm responsible** for
> making sure that my family is okay. I've **always
> expected** that dynamic to include my extended
> family after I was married. **I assumed** that you
> would understand that, but I **did not want to talk
> about it** for fear that you might try to force me to
> choose between my brother and you. **I don't want**
> to lose the close connection to you or to my family,
> but it's difficult because **I feel responsible** for all of
> you. As his brother, **I've expected** to come up with
> the solution and act on it. I just can't figure out how
> to do it because **I feel guilty** about the prospect of
> putting him out.

WHY DO IT THIS WAY?

This conversation offers a window to the expectations that lie beneath each of your behaviors and points of view. When both of you have considered why your expectations of each other don't match, it will be easier to have a different conversation about your agreement, and you'll be more likely to reframe it to reflect that you're a team with a common goal. As you genuinely listen to each other reveal feelings and thoughts, you may feel more assured that you're a priority for your husband, and he can stop taking so much responsibility for so many people around him. As a team, you can figure this out together and reframe it as an issue for the *two* of you, rather than dealing with it like adversaries. This may call for more than one conversation.

Acknowledging the places where you've remained unchanged in your beliefs and assumptions about others might be a clue to finding what is getting in the way. Then you can decide if there are aspects of the existing agreement worth preserving.

The following questions will help you achieve the readiness you need to make this kind of change. Can you answer yes to these?

- Can you shift how you view the silent agreement?

- Are you ready to move out of the cycle of reacting to your relationship woes by creating a narrative that only you know about, while expecting others to live in sync with your narrative?

- Are you ready to reframe this agreement in a way that doesn't blame anyone, using words and behavior that don't push people away? If so, you're ready to begin the task of assessing and reframing.

Keep in mind this is a conscious, intentional change in attitude that maximizes ways to respond to your fears, assert your needs, and create a new dialogue with others. During this process, you're bound to discover new feelings.

Stage 4. Having Courage and Faith

In this stage, you reach for the courage to push beyond the silence and the fears that lie beneath it. You're ready to deal with the situation as it truly is and connect with the other person on a deeper level without shame, fear, or guilt.

HOW TO DO IT

Example—Family Silent Agreement
Now you have a clearer picture of how the silent agreement is causing trouble in an otherwise peaceful marriage. When you decide to have this talk during the phase of courage and faith, you'll rely on the foundation of love and support that you've built over the years, acknowledging that you both hold your relationship dear and that family is important to both of you.

When you are proceeding with courage, you are able to:

- Trust that confronting your silent agreements will strengthen your relationship.

- Believe that although remaining silent may seem more comfortable, communicating openly is a route to genuine resolution.

- See that your silent agreements affect your relationship whether you speak about them or don't, and that uncovering them is a chance for happiness.

WHY DO IT THIS WAY?

Faith and courage will see you through the discomfort of difficult revelations and conflict. Bolster your courage in whatever way works for you.

Now that you understand the basics of resolving a silent agreement, let's delve into the different circumstances that tend to foster silent agreements and explore how you can recognize your own.

CHAPTER 3

SILENT AGREEMENTS ABOUT SEX

A couple's sex life can reveal quite a lot about their relationship. Unfortunately, sex is often the least discussed subject between couples. We often fail to articulate what we want and instead act out our unspoken assumptions, beliefs, and expectations in all kinds of ways. One woman avoids sex by going to bed early while her partner stays up late watching television. In another relationship, one partner meets his sensual needs with someone or something outside the relationship, such as an addiction to pornography. In yet another relationship, sex is mutually satisfying but still rarely spoken about.

A couple's sex life is an arena that lends itself easily to silent agreements because many of us aren't at ease with openly exploring and honestly revealing our sexual needs or inhibitions. Likewise, many of us don't fully understand how we use sex to express feelings and desires. Whether people are or are not aware of their needs or the degree to which they might be sexually dissatisfied, silent agreements often serve to perpetrate dissatisfaction. Sometimes the sex becomes habitual, routine. Maybe the bedroom has become the place where you entertain memories of former lovers so you don't have to address uncomfortable realities like "He can't have an erection anymore" or "She's no longer attracted to me." Or perhaps in the silence you're able to deny the painful truth that the bedroom has become your last refuge against the reality that he's unemployed, that you're a workaholic, or that conversations between you are no longer compelling. Even worse, maybe the passion is so far gone that you don't even fight anymore. In such scenarios, silent agreements often show up and need to be addressed if there's to be any hope of reigniting flames of desire.

If you have a satisfying sex life, don't skip this chapter. Your sex life can change for many reasons—for example, illness, death of a partner, hormonal changes, or employment out of town. Even if your sex life is wonderfully fulfilling, it's important to understand the impact that sex-based silent agreements can have as the years pass and circumstances change. Ask yourself: Is there anything I'm hiding from my partner? If so, do I rationalize that my doing so is "no big deal" or "for his own good"? Using the strategies in this chapter, you'll be unafraid to broach the topic in a productive and loving way.

Because of the many meanings that sex can have for different people and the intense feelings usually present between sexual partners, our sex life is a natural residing place for our expectations and fantasies and for the silent agreements that fuel them. This was the case with Simone and Chandler.

LOVE IN A BUBBLE

Simone and Chandler

Simone, a young, unhappily married professional woman, went on a weeklong Caribbean vacation to de-stress from the demands of her business career, leaving her husband of eight years behind. At the poolside bar a few days before the end of the trip, she met Chandler, a charming and lovable man. Their chemistry was great, and they spent the next three days and nights together talking, laughing, drinking, dancing, and having glorious sex. Their vacation affair looked utterly flawless through their romance-colored glasses. They had so many interests in common! They shared a sense of humor! Their sexual desire for each other was perfectly matched! This gorgeous, kind, patient, interesting, exciting new person gets me! Then it was time to fly home.

Aboard the flight, Simone replayed the previous few days in her mind and wondered if she would ever see Chandler again. She knew she'd just had the sexual adventure of her life. A man of immediate devotion and determination, Chandler felt strongly that Simone was the one. He wanted to rescue her from a demanding life and an unhappy marriage, despite the fact that she had never said a word about wanting to be rescued. He returned home to Paris and fantasized about the life they could share. He felt sure that they were meant to be together, so he decided that very soon he would travel to New York City to reunite with her. And he felt sure that she'd be thrilled to see him.

Chandler arrived in New York and immediately called Simone. She panicked. She was a married woman living with her spouse, and on this day she even had a houseguest—her mother-in-law! What could Chandler have been thinking, flying across the ocean to meet her without her approval? Chandler was expecting Simone to leave her marriage as soon as possible. He thought that she would make an excuse to her husband and that the two lovebirds would spend the weekend at a pricey hotel. Of course this wasn't an option for Simone. While she agreed to have lunch with Chandler, she had no intention of running away with her island lover. She was still "fighting it out" with her husband and she needed to focus. During lunch, she tried to help Chandler understand why she couldn't run away with him, and she feared he wouldn't tolerate being rejected. What if he showed up at her home? Simone knew that she had to be straight with him: She wasn't going to spend the weekend with him and she wasn't going to leave her family. She was terrified of being found out by her husband and family, and during their lunch date, both Chandler and Simone were both terribly tense and nervous. How different the relationship looked under city lights.

WHAT ARE THE SILENT AGREEMENTS?

When Simone and Chandler met, they each carried their own assumptions about sex and love, and they both created silent agreements. These unexpressed wishes and fantasies glided happily alongside one another under the Caribbean sun and shaped a magical three-day encounter. **Simone had secretly resolved that this would be nothing more than a getaway love**, yet she indulged her escape fantasy by acting as if she were available. The moment she stepped off the plane, she projected an air of independence and freedom; in this way she reminded herself that she was sensual and powerful. Chandler was seduced by her free spirit and insatiable desire, and he thought their obvious chemistry signaled that Simone wanted what he wanted. But he resolved to defer discussions about a future until after the trip. **Chandler had a silent agreement to build as much intimacy as possible in their short time together and assumed that it would lead to something long term in the real world. Part of his agreement meant not discussing these hopes with Simone. He didn't want to risk cooling their Caribbean heat.** Sometimes to get what we want, we remain silent, even if it means keeping the truth from the one we most want to be with.

These individual silent agreements led to an enormous discrepancy in their expectations, and their shared silent agreement not to discuss what should happen after the vacation kept the fantasy alive. It was easy for Simone and Chandler to enter silent agreements during their vacation; after all, right away they were mutually attracted, they had similar values, and the fact that they were both writers augmented the fantasy. Both had viewed themselves and each other as "available"; unfortunately for Chandler and his long-term vision, Simone's focus was in the moment. When reality confronted fantasy, fantasy lost. We often trade reality for temporary access to what we need emotionally and sometimes even physically. But what do we do when the truth wakes us up at night?

LIFTING THE SILENCE

Where Do I Start? What Do I Say?
Simone wasn't sure if she wanted to stay in her marriage, but she knew she wasn't ready to leave it. She needed time. And while there wasn't much to be worked out *between* her and Chandler, there was plenty for each of them to learn independently. There might not have been much time for them to discuss what had happened in the Caribbean, but if they had chosen to take the time to individually examine why they entered the affair in the first place, they might have discovered that silent agreements were at the core of it all.

They might begin their conversations with phrases like:

1. I feel . . .
2. I entered the affair because . . .
3. I thought it was clear to you that . . .
4. I assumed that . . .
5. I expected that you would . . .
6. I chose not to talk about it because . . .
7. What I want now is . . .

By looking into their own thoughts and motivations, they can each explore their understanding of what the

Caribbean relationship was relative to their home lives. Simone can examine why she wanted to vacation without her husband, why she was willing to risk her marriage by having an affair, and why she entered into the affair at all. With introspection, she might discover that underlying her marriage are several silent agreements. Do you ever wonder what might loom beneath reckless choices? Often it's not until the thrilling part subsides that we have to face not only what we've done but why. Chandler will need to explore why he was willing to become so emotionally involved with a married person, particularly one who never said that she wanted to leave her husband. And he might come to understand why he was unwilling to talk about what he really wanted with Simone while they were still on the island. Developing this kind of self-awareness might help Chandler avoid repeating such a painful experience. He might even be able to accept the sweetness of the experience and move on—choosing to focus on the beauty of the experience rather than on the pain.

GOING FORWARD

Their story is not uncommon. In fast-moving short-lived affairs, lovers are often too busy making love to acknowledge where their tryst is leading—or where it isn't. Simone can use her memories of the experience to help to figure out what's next for her marriage, while Chandler can use his to help him to better clarify what kind of relationship and communication he wants with a woman who's available.

THE POWER OF SEX

Diana and Troy

While a sexual relationship can offer great opportunity to develop both physical and spiritual intimacy, it can also devolve into a haven for silence, secrecy, and deceit. Sometimes the force of a sexual connection can be so strong that you can feel controlled by it. This magnificent power of sex is a theme that's been explored in literature and song for centuries, and it is often at the heart of drama in various formats. In a popular nighttime television show, for example, the main character tries to disentangle herself from the power of her relationship and laments to her lover, "I wait for you. I watch for you. I can't breathe because I'm waiting for you. You own me. You control me." She's stunned when he replies, "You own *me*. You control *me*. I belong to *you*." The power of their passion makes them each feel like a victim of the other, and they find themselves in a vortex of desire that challenges their ability to forge a relationship built on much else. Underneath, there is a silent agreement that feeds the relationship's sexual power. Troy and Diana have such a story.

Diana was a sophomore in college when she met Troy at a club. He was tall and handsome and had the deepest, sexiest voice she'd ever heard. She was ten years younger than he, and they both loved the age difference. Troy was a custodian at an elementary school while Diana attended an Ivy League university and had plans for graduate education and an ambitious career, but their professional discrepancies didn't deter them. The chemistry was incendiary.

He asked for her number and called her shortly afterward—on New Year's Eve. Though they both had previous engagements, he said that he wanted to come over to see her for just a minute, "just to look at you." It was the sexiest proposition she'd ever heard. He called the next day to tell her how beautiful she was and to suggest that they go to the beach. The beach in winter—she loved how unconventional he was. They had sex that night, and it was intoxicating. And from there the relationship continued—featuring sex and more sex—one month leading to another until nine years passed.

Diana's family said that she would outgrow him. Her friends said he was cool but just "not for her." For Diana, the sex and the intensity of his focus on her drowned out the words of the naysayers. It also helped her forget that she wanted a relationship based on mutual goals, values, morals, and faith. She and Troy had none of these in common. But as long as he soothed her self-doubts and offered to love her, she tolerated the fact that he lacked so much of what she wanted in a man. They had sex twice a day, sometimes more on the weekends. They had nothing in common, but they were in love, and for years they managed to effectively ignore the blatant deficits in their relationship. This "unconscious longevity" isn't all that uncommon. While not facing the truth that the two parts of the couple aren't a fit, people often let years go by before they leave the relationship. This quite often leads to regret.

Wanting Troy to change, Diana began to point out his inadequacies. Meanwhile, he was drinking heavily and using recreational drugs, and while the sex was still wonderful, it occurred with even less communication than ever. Diana began to ache at the idea that with Troy she would never have a relationship of intellectual and emotional equality but would live a life in which she would feel like not much more than a lover. Then Diana accepted a promotion and left New York for Rhode Island. The physical distance between them allowed her to finally acknowledge that she was fooling herself about their future being one of true equals, so she ended the relationship, which broke her heart and his.

WHAT ARE THE SILENT AGREEMENTS?

Diana silently agreed to ignore that her relationship with Troy was imbalanced in the ways that mattered to her. She agreed to focus instead on being in love and having the fiery sex life that distracted her while hoping that the rest would simply change for the better. In fact, Diana had always wanted to feel passionately desired by a sexually hungry man who was madly in love with her. She believed that attracting a man through sensuality and sex would ensure his love. It seemed to work for her friends! Unfortunately, she learned that having a relationship with Troy meant that she wasn't going to have the other things she wanted—certainly not intellectual companionship. She silently hoped that their sex-based relationship would grow into a relationship of depth and compatibility. It didn't.

Troy silently agreed to ignore Diana's need for a different kind of relationship and instead kept showing his love by making love. He spent much of his time doing things that made him comfortable: going to baseball games where he could teach Diana the game, taking her to the

movies, or just hanging out on the stoop smoking a ciga-
rette. He ignored his silent desire to continue his education and instead gave into his fear of personal growth. The
more Troy learned about Diana and her family, the more
he realized that she wanted a different kind of man. But
he wasn't trying to grow, to explore how his dreams might
fit with hers. Too many years had intervened between him
and his dreams; instead, he focused on making her sexually happy because that's all he could give her. Troy defi-
nitely didn't want to admit his fears of inadequacy. If he
went back to school to try to better himself, he might fail
and, in the meantime, lose his pension. It's an often-told
tale: Fear stops a person from reaching for something that
could make him truly happy. That fear of failure fortified
his silent agreement with himself: to walk the safe road of
complacency in exchange for protection from the kinds of
failures that might drive him to a serious dependence on
alcohol and drugs.

LIFTING THE SILENCE

Where Do I Start? What Do I Say?

There are all kinds of breakups. Some relationships end
with a whimper, some linger until the lights flicker out,
and others go out with a bang! However the relationship
ends, there are silent agreements underlying its demise.
If you're like Diana and you feel it both safe and valuable
to discuss the relationship with the person you're leaving,
you'll first want to explore your own silent agreements.
As always, at the root of the agreements are underlying assumptions, expectations, and fears that lead to a

willingness to enter the silent agreement in the first place. Understanding the origins of a silent agreement doesn't always happen right away, but using specific exploratory language is a crucial first step.

Try this: Focus on the relationship in question, and with the goal of understanding what helped create and perpetrate the silence, finish these sentences (and feel free to create others in this vein):

1. I feel . . .
2. I have always believed . . .
3. I was raised to think that . . .
4. I assumed that . . .
5. I expected that you would . . .
6. I've been afraid to talk about this because . . .
7. What I want now is . . .

For Diana, some of these sentences completed might sound like this: **I feel** frustrated that our relationship's love and our passionate sexual connection aren't leading to more compatibility. **I have always believed** that I would spend my life with someone who thought he was equal to me. **I have also always believed** that for a relationship to be satisfying, there needs to be sensual and sexual passion and excitement and that I have to be deeply desired by a man, and Troy and I had that! **I assumed that** my relationship with Troy would grow beyond the sexually dominated dynamic of our early months together while retaining the deep love we had for each other. **I've been afraid to talk about this because** maybe then I'd have to admit that I knew it wasn't going to change. And maybe

I'd have to admit how responsible I am for letting it go on for so long. **What I want now is** a healthy, loving life with a man who feels like an equal—sexually, intellectually, and emotionally.

Once Diana gained the clarity and strength to admit to herself that she wanted out of the relationship, she vowed to make sure that her communication with Troy would be clear, strong, and sensitive. When you're in this kind of situation, much of the language that you used in your conversation with yourself will be effective in your conversation with the other person. Keep in mind that defensiveness is a big barrier to progress, so always try to use language that doesn't blame or accuse the other. Avoid phrases like *you should, you didn't,* and *you never.* Be brave and speak from the heart about how you feel.

When you want to lift the silence, consider using some of these phrase starters:

1. I feel that . . .
2. I've assumed that . . .
3. I think I've avoided talking about this because . . .
4. My concern is . . .
5. I would like to . . .
6. Going forward, I hope that . . .

During the conversation, try to respond with sentiments that validate the other person's feelings and thoughts:

1. I can understand why you see it that way.
2. You make a good point.

3. I hear you.
4. I've had a similar feeling, but I haven't known how to address it.
5. I do love you. Still, I think this conversation is necessary to keep us from further hurt.

You can also solicit the other person's ideas and feelings with questions that begin like:

1. What do you think about that?
2. Does this come as a surprise to you?
3. Does this make sense to you?
4. Do you see how we've both participated in this?

GOING FORWARD

After nine years that included a number of attempts to fix what was wrong, Diana knew that the relationship would never become what she wanted, so she felt she had no choice but to free herself and Troy. She ended the relationship, and that's when she began to understand that the silent agreement she'd been living within was one she'd created many years before. If she's honest with herself, she'll see that she had glimpses of the silent agreement all along, but many years had to pass before she could acknowledge how the agreement was disrupting her life and her happiness. If Diana had continued to "live silently," it's likely that she would have become bitter, feeling that she'd wasted her prime years on something that wasn't going anywhere. Given the kind of future that Diana clearly wanted, eliminating the silent agreement from her life was the right decision. She learned that sexual fireworks don't necessarily feed the love over time. More depth is necessary to lead to the kind of relationship she wants long term. That's not to say that she won't have a passionate love life with a man who shares her values and her level of curiosity. Finding more of a balance is entirely possible. Now she knows that she mustn't let the sex convince her to ignore what's missing. A passionate sex life and love that took her breath away left her very satisfied in the short term. But she began to feel emotionally and intellectually unsatisfied. In the future, if she learns important lessons from this heartbreak, she'll be much better prepared to spot the signs if her sex life is hiding some important truths.

Troy is also now in a position to choose differently. He was half of the fantasy. He immersed himself in the love and the sexual aspects of the relationship to avoid thinking or talking about the fact that he felt the gap between her needs and his ability to meet them. Keeping the focus on what they did well together helped him feel that he was enough and assuaged his fears of being rejected. Now that Diana lifted the silence, Troy has countless options to consider: (1) He can face his fears about personal growth in an environment without judgment. (2) He can try to find a woman who doesn't want more than he has to offer. (3) Without first learning to challenge himself, he can pursue a woman who's similar to Diana and risk repeating his pattern.

Option 2 could lead him to contentment in a relationship that doesn't demand much of him, but that might lead him eventually to boredom. Option 3 would involve choosing another woman like Diana with whom he might experience an exciting period of steamy sex and love followed by the sight of another ambitious woman walking out the door. But, Option 1 could be the one that allows him to reach for his dreams now that they are out in the open.

After an agreement is no longer silent, both people have the option to learn from the experience and make better choices in the future.

SILENT AGREEMENTS THAT KILL YOUR SEX LIFE

While there are often legitimate reasons for sexual time-outs in relationships, such breaks can be signs of hidden silent agreements. There are many couples whose lack of sex can't be explained by hormonal problems, low sex drive, or physical or mental illness. In these cases, the lack of a sex life is rooted in silent agreements. Quite often, people will express their silent agreements through avoidance of sex; for them, avoiding sexual closeness protects them from vulnerability and exposure. But when people minimize or even ignore problems that exist between them, sex can disappear for weeks, months, and even years. By avoiding sex, they might be trying to mask problems of intimacy or control, and this kind of aversion is most often based in some kind of fear. Put simply: "If I don't get naked, I won't have to feel naked."

TOO DOWN TO GET DOWN

In this scenario, both of you are depressed. Often in this kind of situation, whether or not either party understands that depression has invaded the relationship, neither is trying to do anything about it. Of course, depression causes us to lose interest in things that we normally enjoy, and sex can be one of those things. You might justify a loss of sexual intimacy by saying to yourselves: "The honeymoon is over. That's normal for a five-year relationship, right?" Because you're agreeing not to acknowledge the depression, you're giving yourselves permission to ignore your sadness about the loss of your sex life. Accepting the lack of fireworks keeps you from dealing with the fact that even when you're depressed, *you* have to do something to make it better.

WHAT HAPPENED TO THE PERSON I MARRIED?

Kenny and Maya

Meet Kenny and Maya, a couple for whom sex has become a distant memory. Kenny, an accountant, and Maya, a former actress and now a schoolteacher, were childhood sweethearts who have now been married for eleven years. They share a pleasant, comfortable life that includes two young children, a house, two cats, a dog, good friends, and loving relatives. Their life together is full, and they share many happy moments. But they don't make love anymore.

In the beginning, they were attracted to each other's enthusiasm and sense of adventure. Maya dreamed of becoming a famous actress, a phenomenon on the Broadway stage. Kenny, a bright, funny, and energetic guy, has a creative mind and dreamed of starting several innovative businesses that the world would beat a path to. However, he was a dutiful son and followed his parents' advice in college to choose a major that would ensure that he could always find a job.

They married right after college and soon had their children, two rambunctious girls. Maya put her acting career on hold, and Kenny delayed realizing his entrepreneurial dreams to make sure that his family had everything they needed. Eleven years later, their lives were very different from the exciting adventure they had pictured. They didn't talk about the turn life had taken, so silent agreements developed between them. Now these agreements have stifled their sex life and threatened their marriage.

Maya wants to have sex with her husband, but he just doesn't seem interested anymore. She tells herself to be patient, to light some candles, to wear sexy lingerie. Nothing works. Maya used to try to talk to Kenny about it, often offering excuses for him right away: "Honey, I know you've been working really hard lately, but . . ." But the conversations never went far. Kenny, a good guy who loves his wife, would deny that he felt overworked or overtired. He'd smile and tell her, "Baby, relax. We'll get to it. We're fine." Maya became confused as she listened to her girlfriends describe their lagging sex lives; *they* were always the ones who tried to avoid sex. Kenny's assurances would give Maya a sense of hope. She'd tell herself she was pressuring Kenny too much and that she did indeed need to relax. Then another sexless month or two would go by. Finally Maya admitted that she was more than just sex-starved. Now she was just plain angry.

WHAT ARE THE SILENT AGREEMENTS?

Silent agreements that are expressed through passionate sex (or through its absence) often call attention to themselves sooner than other kinds of silent agreements because of the vulnerability and intimacy involved. Maya and Kenny's sensual and sexual time-out was a clear signal that what had been unspoken between them was trying to find a voice. **Maya had silently agreed that because she was blessed with a wonderful family life, she had no right to complain about her sex life.** This agreement was a reflection of her harsh upbringing during which, whenever she asked for more than she had, she had been told that she was "selfish and ungrateful." People often reminded her that Kenny was a dream husband and she convinced herself that an unselfish wife doesn't complain about her sex life when everything else is wonderful. Meanwhile, Kenny kept Maya on hold by sweetly promising that things would be normal again "soon." Maya began to feel dismissed, and she was uncomfortable boldly admitting that the neglect of her body was breaking her heart.

Kenny had an agreement with himself to be as good a husband and father as his own father had been, a man who often said, "A real man doesn't let his feelings get in the way of his responsibilities." He focused on being a good husband despite his anxiety about a marriage in which he was unhappy and unfulfilled. Kenny internalized this belief from his childhood days of rushing home from school to babysit his brothers while his parents were at work. He'd had no choice then. How he felt about his responsibilities didn't seem to matter to his parents, and he carried those "stuffed feelings" and beliefs about having no choice into his silent agreement with the woman he loved. Although he loved Maya and didn't want to lose her, he had never dreamed that his life with her could become so very predictable. Saddened by their inability to forge a stimulating marriage and dismayed by Maya's seeming acceptance of the traditional marriage they had settled into, Kenny became distant. And sometimes when he did engage sexually, he was unable to perform. What Kenny discovered was that his withholding of sex gave him a sense of control over a situation that seemed otherwise out of his hands.

This is an interesting aspect of how silent agreements work. While they can make you miserable, they can also offer secondhand perks, such as a feeling of being in control. The longer Kenny refrained from sex with his wife, the longer he was able to feel like the boss of at least one aspect of his life. And by withholding sex, he got to silently express his anger at Maya for morphing into a settled suburban wife—so different from the feisty, free-spirited young woman he had fallen in love with. When she did express anger about their lack of sex, he became excited that she might once again become that passionate and surprising woman he fell in love with years ago. For Maya, the perk was she could let go of the notion that Kenny was perfect; he wasn't being her lover anymore, so *perfect* couldn't be applied to him. Now that he was no longer a flawless husband in her eyes, she could let go of her need to be a perfect lover and housewife. And a less perfect image of Kenny made her feel less anxious about reviving her earlier unconventional career as a full-time actress. This aspirational dream had been buried in their pursuit of the "perfect" suburban life. Clearly, the perks didn't compensate for their lack of a sex life, but that's the irony of silent agreements: They can become part of the fabric of your relationship in ways that scream trouble, all the while serving some other unexpressed underlying need. If the silence is lifted (and the agreement revealed), the couple can begin to forge a life together that exemplifies what they truly want—love and happiness with a healthy sex life.

LIFTING THE SILENCE

Where Do I Start? What Do I Say?
Again, before discussing a silent agreement with a partner, we should first look inward. The first step is to take an honest look at your own underlying assumptions, expectations, fears, and insecurities that led to your willingness to sustain the silence. Understanding the origins of a silent agreement doesn't always happen right away, but using specific exploratory thinking as you embark on conversations with open minds and common language is a crucial first step.

Try this: Finish the sentences you found on page 50. Focus on the relationship in question with the goal of understanding what helped create and perpetuate the silence.

For Maya, some of these sentences completed might sound like this: **I feel** frustrated and shut out. **I have always believed** that a marriage should include a passionate sex life. **I have also always believed** that a woman who has a kind and loyal husband and healthy, happy kids is a very fortunate woman. **I assumed that** if our sex life ever began to fade, my husband would really want to change that. **I've been afraid to talk about this because** I don't want to make Kenny angry or make him want to push me away even more. **What I want now is** regular and brave communication about what goes on and doesn't go on between us. **What I want now** is a healthy, loving sex life.

After you've explored your own perception of the silent agreement and you're ready to talk, there are many ways to begin a conversation with your partner. The conversation could start with an invitation: "Let's talk for just five minutes." A first conversation might seem less intimidating if you agree to keep it short.

When you want to lift the silence, consider using some of the following basic phrase starters found in the earlier part of the chapter:

1. I feel that . . .
2. I've assumed that . . .
3. I think I've avoided talking about this because . . .
4. My concern is . . .
5. I would like to . . .
6. Going forward, I hope that . . .

Remember to respond with sentiments that validate the other person's feelings and thoughts:

1. I can understand why you see it that way.
2. That's a new idea for me. I'm going to give that some thought.
3. You make a good point.
4. I hear you.
5. I've had a similar feeling, but I haven't known how to address it.

Don't forget to solicit the other person's ideas and feelings with questions that begin like:

1. What do you think about that?
2. Does this come as a surprise to you?
3. How can I support you in this?
4. Does this make sense to you?
5. Do you have some ideas about how we can make changes that will be good for both of us?

And remember, your silent agreement didn't develop in a single day and probably won't be resolved that quickly either. Be sensitive to discussion fatigue, and feel free to offer to wrap up the first conversation so that each of you can take some time to process what you've learned. One or more conversations might be ahead, but for many people the first one is the most challenging, so cheers to you for taking such a positive step.

GOING FORWARD

Maya certainly didn't want an end to her marriage; she wanted an end to the sexual drought. But her previous attempts to revive their love life hadn't been enough—she kept gently asking and Kenny kept gently refusing. The agreement was a cover for their fears about not being able to have the kind of life they longed for, individually and together. If they continued to adhere to their silent agreements, the suffering would present in two forms: They wouldn't get to live the kind of day-to-day life they want, and they also wouldn't get to have sex. The best solution would involve their agreeing to talk about problems in their sex life as soon as they arise, and that required the start of a potentially uncomfortable talk.

A healthy sex life has communication at its core. Couples should check in with each other regularly about how each is feeling about the relationship because silence can turn an issue that was once small and relatively simple into one that's large and very complex. Do you know if your partner is feeling bored, angry, or frustrated? Do you want your partner to hear about your needs that aren't being met? Are you keeping negative thoughts to yourself to avoid a confrontation? Are you simply focusing on other things to avoid having the conversation? Are you acting out your feelings without sharing the conversations going on in your mind? Are you numbing the feelings or completely shutting them down?

We get better at things we practice well, so couples who regularly discuss their feelings, hopes, doubts, and needs will likely find such conversations easier and easier over time. After Maya and Kenny began really communicating, they not only began to genuinely hear what the other wanted but were able to acknowledge their actions toward each other and stop the behaviors that were sabotaging the relationship. As a result, they experienced rewards well beyond the resurgence of their sex life. Maya felt free to rethink her career dreams because she no longer felt trapped by the idea that she was supposed to live a traditional suburban life with all the sexual limitations she hadn't imagined would go with it. This change in Maya was exciting to Kenny, which added to their sexual happiness. Their new open communication helped Kenny to feel less pressured to be perfect, even as a lover. He too had been following a path that he hadn't chosen for himself as a husband or a parent. Kenny needed to feel free to define *husband* and *father* on his own terms, and now that he and Maya were being open about expectations, desires, and dreams, he was much freer to do so—now with the support of his partner.

MIDDLE AGE AND BEYOND

Is a Sex Life Still Part of the Picture?

Perhaps. It's really up to you. If you are middle-aged or beyond, you might find that you're not getting as many looks as you used to, which may feel disappointing at first. Make sure not to devalue yourself. Just remember you're an older and wiser fish swimming in a new pond. Walk the runway of life! Now is the time to live out loud without falling into unhealthy silent agreements.

. . .

Meet Gwen. She's middle-aged, and she's in a predicament. She has two grown children, one grandson, and an increasing sense of loneliness. With retirement looming, she worries about becoming even lonelier. She hasn't had a lover in years and is afraid that she never will again. Divorced at age thirty, she became the sole provider for her sons. During those years, she went back to school to become a teacher and lived paycheck to paycheck to support her boys and maintain their modest home in a safe neighborhood. Sometimes she would wistfully think about romance, but as she focused on the demands of her life, the thoughts would pass.

While Gwen dated and traveled occasionally on her own, she never met a man she felt comfortable introducing to her boys. Her brief affair with an unhappily married neighbor ended in disaster and she avoided love after that. She lost all confidence in herself as a desirable woman, but now, years later, Gwen is reconsidering her future. She wants a love life, but she has long been absent from the dating world and lacks confidence, so how can she make it happen?

During a book club meeting, she asked her friends for advice. They offered creative ideas that included going to church socials, volunteering, traveling, and looking up lost loves. Many of her friends were also online dating, and they encouraged her to create a profile and give it a try. That's when Gwen perked up. What had she been waiting for? It was time to reinvent herself and embrace her reawakening sexual self. With the support of her friends, she began to take weekly salsa lessons and stretch classes and found excellent plus-size lingerie stores. She even had a cosmetic makeover. Gwen was finally having fun and it showed! She became aware that men were noticing her, and she liked it.

When she met Lewis, she felt the click. Lewis had five grandchildren and was recently retired. Yes, he was balding and a bit overweight, and yes, he needed to update his wardrobe and he couldn't see five feet ahead without his glasses, but he was a thoughtful, funny, caring guy who was available and attracted to her. They overcame all obstacles in bed. Romantic lighting, music, and playful outfits enhanced their steamy encounters. While lovemaking was not as frequent as she might have liked, Lewis made up for it with his loving disposition. They got along beautifully, made each other laugh, and took care of each other from that day on. Gwen had never been happier. She finally had a real partner to play with both inside and outside the bedroom.

WHAT IS THE SILENT AGREEMENT?

While raising her sons, Gwen had silently agreed with herself that motherhood would be enough to satisfy her. She gave the impression that she had no other needs beyond being a devoted mother and schoolteacher, and she chose to ignore her sexual self for many years. If she continued to be a long-standing sufferer, the martyr who focused only on her own children, her life would be limited to the stories she told herself about middle age and love. Sure, she would enjoy her grandchildren and her relationships with her adult sons, but she would always know that she was neglecting a very important part of being a woman, and that would lead to regret.

LIFTING THE SILENCE

Where Do I Start? What Do I Say?
Someone like Gwen who is trying to emerge from a long drought needs to start by acknowledging the need for a more satisfying life. Parenting and grandparenting are big responsibilities and wonderful, deeply enriching endeavors, but there can be more to life. If you've set your needs aside for too long and are now searching for a more sexual life, you must first examine what you want and why you haven't given those desires priority before now. Your conversation with yourself might involve turning these phrases into sentences that reflect a new self-understanding:

1. I feel . . .
2. I thought that to be a good parent . . .
3. Not having a sex life all these years has meant . . .
4. I assumed that . . .
5. I was afraid that . . .
6. I chose not to try to change my sexual situation because . . .
7. What I want now is . . .

When we're honest with ourselves about how and why we enter into and then remain in certain situations and patterns, we gain a clearer understanding of our silent agreements. And when we can see where those agreements came from, we're more likely to be able to avoid such silences in the future.

GOING FORWARD

Gwen had to change, and change she did. With the help of her friends, she realized that it was time to do something about her need for romance, sex, and all the fun that goes with them. She had to bypass her fears about her weight, her age, and her years out of the dating game. She just had to give it a try. When she began to embrace the possibility of having a vibrant relationship again, she was able to shed her old silent agreement and its signature martyrdom. Her new agreement focused on appreciating all she had accomplished, while vowing to move through life as a woman who expected to live fully as an interesting, fun, and sexual being. With her new verve for life, Gwen was able to find a companion who embraced life in the same way.

POWER AND CONTROL: SEX AS A WEAPON

Too often, sex is used as a bargaining chip in relationships. In this scenario, you're angry at your partner, and rather than address the issue directly, you punish him or her by withholding sex. Forgiveness doesn't come easily to you, and you have a silent agreement that people should pay for their wrongdoings, so you wield that power by freezing the other person out in the bedroom. In this silent agreement, you continue on without sex, making excuses like "I just don't feel sexual lately" or "He just isn't doing it for me."

Your partner may also be keeping quiet on the other side of your silent agreement. His own silent agreement might be to refuse to admit that he's upset by the freeze-out because such an admission might be interpreted as being needy and that would mean conceding control to you. In this case, your silent agreements are perfectly aligned to keep your sex life dormant; you're punishing him for what you feel he has done wrong by withholding sex, and he isn't about to beg. This stalemate can go on indefinitely.

When you want to lift the silence, consider using some of the following phrase starters we've discussed:

1. Maybe it's me, but . . .
2. Is there a different way for us to talk about this?
3. I think I've avoided talking about this because . . .
4. My real concern is . . .
5. Tell me where you are coming from . . .
6. Going forward, can we do more of . . .

As always, try to respond with sentiments that validate the other person's feelings and thoughts:

1. I can understand why you see it that way.
2. You make a good point.
3. I hear you.
4. I've had a similar feeling, but I haven't known how to address it.

Remember to engage the other person's ideas and feelings with questions that begin like:

1. What do you think about that?
2. Does this come as a surprise to you?
3. Does this make sense to you?
4. Do you see how we've both participated in this?

Dysfunctional silent agreements work together like sinister partners who want to keep your bedroom a cold and lonely place. Whether you're the one punishing your partner or the one being punished, do your best to look past the insults and hurts enough to start conversations that will lift the silence.

THE MARTYR AND THE MEANIE: HIDING THE REAL ISSUE

The Martyr and the Meanie scenario often emerges when you and your partner can't handle the idea of being both angry with and close to each other at the same time. In this scenario, the "Meanie" acts out the anger of both parties about an unacknowledged issue by withholding sex. Such a situation can emerge if the person who acts as the Martyr is afraid to reveal the intensity of her own anger. Instead, she silently agrees to let her partner display the anger for both of them by denying them both sex. At the same time, the person cast as the Meanie might have trouble expressing his tender side. After all, he's not *all* about anger, and he does still love her. But for him, to demonstrate his anger in a disguised form might feel less intimidating than to reveal it outright; such a revelation might include admitting the terrifying idea that he fears he might fail her as a partner. So he withholds sex while she martyrs herself to the cause and tolerates the sexual drought. And so their silent agreement remains intact.

In this situation, there's a lot going on beneath the surface. The Martyr and the Meanie dynamic isn't about power; it's about disavowed feelings. Only one partner gets to manifest the anger that exists between them while the other does not. This dynamic allows them to achieve their mutual goal of avoiding the larger issues between them.

Clearly, silent agreements in the sexual arena that are left unaddressed can lead to frustration, disappointment, and derailed relationships. The impact that they can have on our sex lives—the loss of intimacy and pleasure, as well as our sense of well-being and downright fun—cannot be ignored. So, keep talking, reaching out, and looking within.

CHAPTER 4

SILENT AGREEMENTS ABOUT MONEY

Our views about money incite feelings that may have nothing to do with how many financial assets we have. Instead, they have everything to do with upbringing, self-perception, and issues related to love, security, independence, power, and control. Many of us give little thought to why we use money as we do. But we often make decisions and act out unspoken feelings through our use of money. Sometimes these unspoken feelings have no impact on financial circumstances. At other times, they lead to silent agreements that undermine not only our finances but also our relationships with our romantic partners, with our colleagues, and even the relationship we have with ourselves. Sometimes the ramifications of such silent agreements can be dramatic. Certainly, this was the case for Tina and Doug. As you read about their struggles, you may recognize strains of your own relationships in the way that these two clash without really having a sense of what the other person is expecting, believing, or experiencing when it comes to money.

NOW I UNDERSTAND

Tina and Doug

Tina and Doug met in college at a football game where his fraternity and her sorority were stepping for the halftime show. The air was filled with the thundering rhythm of their routines, and their hearts felt alive with the promise of "anything can happen." Tina and Doug were instantly taken with each other. As they talked, they felt the rush of attraction and the delight of discovering that they had many things in common: Both were athletic, church-going, and known for their laughter. Almost immediately, they felt the thrilling click that hinted, "This might be the one." Then, after six years of dances, trips, dates, family reunions, and movie nights curled up together on a couch, they were married.

The first five years of the marriage were blissful. Tina began to follow the career path she'd outlined back when they would lie on the beach and share their dreams for the future. She finished her master's degree in education, taught school for several years, and eventually was promoted to principal. She was well respected, earned a good salary, and was firmly moving along the career path that she had defined for herself.

Doug's story was very different. An entrepreneur at heart, he pursued his dream of owning a business. He took postgrad business courses and partnered with several friends to develop ideas. Over the next ten years, he started a home painting company, a general contracting company, a moving company, and several other endeavors that he didn't stay with very long. Every eighteen months or so he came up with a "bigger and better" idea. Doug had always been the kind of guy who liked new things—new jobs, new classes, new projects. He was energized by change.

Meanwhile, they had two children and bought a house anchored by a big mortgage. In the early years, Tina had been content with their life, and she'd been Doug's biggest champion, always hoping that sooner or later he'd settle on a professional pursuit that would hold his attention. But after ten years, neither could deny the strain on their marriage. Countless arguments about Doug's business vision seemed to lead nowhere, and eventually they stopped talking about it altogether. Tina grew quietly bitter. The two spent less and less time together, and their sex life all but disappeared. Tina told her husband (and herself) that she was simply exhausted because of work demands. Doug started hanging out at the local bar, where he drank more than usual and flirted with women. One night when Doug came in late from the bar, he found Tina sitting in the dark, and neither could answer the question "How did we get here?"

WHAT ARE THE SILENT AGREEMENTS?

Both Doug's and Tina's aspirations and fears created the perfect backdrop for their silent agreements, one of which read like this: **Doug avoided fear of failure by silently agreeing to deny the possibility that his business ventures**

might never succeed. Despite the financial difficulties that Doug's unsuccessful business ventures posed to their family, Tina had been a party to this agreement. For ten years she remained silent about her fear that Doug would never be an equal financial partner. **They both also silently agreed that Tina would support Doug's ventures and that this would prove her to be a special woman who always stood by her man.** This part of the silent agreement was especially powerful for Tina and Doug because they both believed it would ultimately save their relationship in the event that Doug continued to struggle professionally.

LIFTING THE SILENCE

As dismal as this scenario may seem, maybe you're getting a sense of how these two landed here. Have you been fighting the same fight with your partners, friends, or family? It's not uncommon to find yourself in relationships where you're the responsible one while the other constantly forgets his or her wallet, neglects to pay you back, or looks to you to fund the family outing. This is the time to try to unveil your silent agreement with yourself as well as the one you have with others. Is being the responsible one something that rewards you somehow? Maybe you don't like paying for everything and complain about it, but your silent agreement with yourself won't let you stop because you like being the one who has the means to do it. Asking yourself the simple question "What am I getting out of this?" can help you begin to understand that you have a silent agreement with yourself that's part of the dynamic between you and your freeloading friends, family, or mate. Of course, maintaining this dynamic takes two, so the other parties will need to explore what is unspoken on their end. Maybe they have a silent agreement to get their needs met through others, to avoid failure by not trying in the first place, or to act out their envy of your financial success by letting you pay for everything—take *that*, Miss Fancy Pants! Whatever underlies the intersection of the silent agreements you have with yourself and each other, the first step is always to look within.

When we think about what may be under the surface with Tina and Doug, we can see that they had similar ideas about the lifestyle they wanted, and they expected to create it as a team. Tina's plan involved a structured, predictable career path that assured financial security. Doug, on the other hand, had dreams of mega-success as an entrepreneur by way of an undefined path. Tina's steady income eased his fears as he chased his dreams. But he never dreamed that Tina would lose faith in him.

Tina was especially sensitive to her role as supporter because she'd grown up in a family of women who seemed contemptuous of their men. She vowed that she would choose a man she could believe in and would support him all the way. However, she hadn't been clear with herself or Doug about how far her support would extend if Doug's professional life didn't take off. She'd never thought it would become an issue.

FIRST STEPS: WHAT'S BEHIND MY SILENT AGREEMENT?

How then do you proceed when you're caught in the middle of a silent agreement about money? Even better, how do you prevent yourself from being caught in the first place? As we noted above, the first step is to look within and try to uncover some of the beliefs and expectations you have about money that may be surfacing in your relationships. The following exercise will help you to gain a clearer picture of what is informing your silent agreements and will lay the groundwork for the conversations to follow.

Directions: Fill out your responses to each question below in the corresponding section of the Money Pie. Be sure to include your thoughts and feelings in each area. Try not to censor yourself; no answer is right or wrong, good or bad. You'll end up with a better sense of your silent agreements if you're candid about your agreements while doing this exercise.

Beliefs and Feelings

1. What I heard and saw about money while growing up
2. What I felt and thought about money while growing up

3. If I had a million dollars and lost it, what might be my thoughts and feelings?
4. If I lost a million dollars but not the things that matter most to me, what might be my thoughts and feelings?

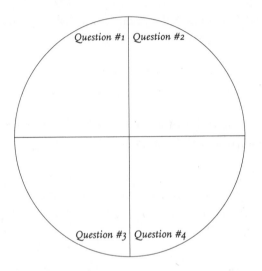

For example, here are some responses from Tina's pie:

What I heard and saw about money while growing up: Become a professional, have a steady job, live a comfortable life.

What I felt and thought about money while growing up: It's the source of marital conflict and unhappiness.

If I had a million dollars and lost it, what might be my thoughts and feelings? I would be devastated.

What if I lost a million dollars but not the things that matter most to me? As long as I had my family I would be okay.

While Doug's pie might look like this:

What I heard and saw about money while growing up: Working a job won't get you the life you want.

What I felt and thought about money while growing up: I want more.

If I had a million dollars and lost it, what might be my thoughts and feelings? I would fight to regain all that I lost.

What if I lost a million dollars but not the things that matter most to me? I would feel that I failed my family.

Now fill out your own pie. Take your time so you can look beneath the surface.

Finally, respond to the questions below to help you round out the picture of what's in your silent agreements about money.

Expectations and Assumptions

Hint: Think about whether and how your answers are linked.

How closely does my current financial picture match my ideal (on a scale of 1 to 10)?

What would I need/expect from my partner to establish my ideal financial picture?

After you and your partner have completed this exercise individually, you can discuss your answers together. Or can you? Getting to the heart of silent agreements means finding the courage to talk about finances as well as feelings. In the case of Tina and Doug, they had become so angry that constructive conversation was difficult to initiate and sustain. You might find yourself in a similar predicament because money issues between people are usually loaded and can invoke a lot of intense feelings. That's why it's important to first create an atmosphere where both parties feel safe to discuss their silent fears and concerns without criticism and judgment. When you embark on these conversations, you can prepare by following a few guidelines.

INDIVIDUALLY

Record answers to the following:

- What do I want to gain from this conversation? (Be specific.)

- What am I willing to give to this conversation? (Be specific.)

- What fears do I have about being open and candid?

- What do I need from my partner to help me be open and candid? (Identify something specific that your partner can do.)

- What can I offer my partner to help him/her be open and candid? (Identify something specific that you can do.)

- Write a list of three statements that counter the criticisms/judgments you've had of your partner.

TOGETHER

- Choose a time to have the conversation when you're not likely to be tired, distracted, or interrupted. For example, hire a babysitter; turn off your phone and other technology; meet in a quiet, neutral space; and listen to each other.

- Define your listening rules. For example, you may want to take turns giving each other five minutes to talk without interruption.

- Designate a time limit for this conversation. This is important to help you avoid "summit fatigue." You can schedule a follow-up conversation, if you like.

PREPARING FOR THE CONVERSATION

- Share your answers to the questions above with your partner.

- Ask questions about your partner's answers.

- Restate your partner's answers to confirm that you understand.

- Do your best to communicate in ways that encourage your partner's most openhearted responses. Examples might sound like this: "I am hearing you say that . . ." "Am I getting what you're saying?" "Is there more to it that I should understand?" "It's helpful to get your perspective."

THE CONVERSATION

Once you and your partner have set the stage for safe and open communication, it's time to uncover the silent agreements that may be disrupting your relationship. You can now discuss all that you have discovered as you filled out your Money Pie. The conversation in this part of the exercise might be geared to help reveal how what you saw or heard growing up is reflected in how you spend, save, make, and/or lose money. While discussing your answers, you're likely to find it easier to identify deeper beliefs and feelings about having or not having money as well as what kind of role you expect money to play in your life. The discussion should also help to clarify which other aspects of your life you value. For example, Tina and Doug might discover that they mutually value family above all else, but that large sums of money mean different things to each of them. This could help their overall understanding of how they each respond differently to Doug's entrepreneurial struggles.

What are some things that both you and your partner value that could help you come together over your differences about money? Armed with the insights that you're likely to gain from your discussion, examine where you and your partner stand in regard to your desired financial picture. This includes exploring obstacles that appear to be in the way of your ideal scenario. If you haven't been able to do so already, during this process you're likely to uncover your silent agreements about money. The obstacles you face often tell the story of where your silent agreements are in alignment and where they don't match. You can better recognize such a discrepancy by studying how well your *behaviors* match what you believe or expect from yourself and from your partner when it comes to dealing with money. Consider the following:

- In what ways does your behavior match or depart from your beliefs about how money should be handled?

- In what ways does your partner's behavior match or depart from your beliefs about how money should be handled?

- In what ways does your behavior match or not match your expectations of yourself about making and/or keeping money? For example, "I expect to earn a considerable salary increase each year, but my partner makes a good salary, so I stay in a job that offers only small raises."

- In what ways does your partner's behavior match or not match your expectations of him/her about making and/or keeping money? For example, "I expect her to maintain a steady income and contribute equally, but she keeps changing jobs and comes up short."

If you like visuals, charting your matches and mismatches can sometimes help you understand where you and your partner are in or out of alignment. It can illuminate what you've been silently agreeing to and in which ways those agreements may be unworkable or even unhealthy. Exploring your silent agreements in this format also helps you develop a sense of unity as you work together to create a visual representation of how your relationship came to be disrupted by your silent agreements about money. You can also keep a copy of your chart of expectations to refer to if you find yourself slipping into old disagreements and frustrations about your financial relationship. This chart allows you to see a cross section of your beliefs and your behavior.

	MY BELIEFS	MY EXPECTATIONS
MY BEHAVIOR		
MY PARTNER'S BEHAVIOR		

GOING FORWARD

Many struggles about money reflect other issues that may be difficult to identify or discuss, so uncovering your silent agreements about money can forge greater overall understanding of your partner. For Doug and Tina, digging deeper and exploring the issues behind their assumptions allowed them both to identify what they valued and to have more compassion for each other. Tina was able to share her feelings about the women in her family. She had felt anxious and sad as she witnessed her father and favorite uncles being treated with disrespect by their wives. She was close to her father, a loving and kind man, and her mother's strident behavior toward him made Tina fear that he would leave them one day. The same fear kept her silent for years while Doug was floundering.

Understanding Tina's history, Doug reassured her that his commitment to her was solid. By exploring his own upbringing, Doug came to understand himself on a deeper level. His father and other men in his community worked long, hard hours in the local factory but never achieved financial success. He didn't want that kind of life and vowed to become successful even though he was extremely unsure of himself and afraid that he might not do any better than the men in his father's circle. But Doug believed that a good wife's role was to support her man's efforts, no matter what.

When Tina and Doug had a better understanding of themselves and each other, they were able to reframe their silent agreement, and of course eliminate the silence. Tina was able to assert that she expected Doug to work and contribute his share, and if he failed to do so, she reserved the right to speak up without reserve. She helped Doug to see that expressing her concerns as they developed was a form of support that would help them come to a better agreement together. At the same time, Doug identified specific goals for his business, including time frames and the amount of money he would contribute to the family bank account while getting his business off the ground. Seeing that he still had Tina's support, Doug felt more motivated to be clear about his efforts. Ultimately, Doug wanted to be able to ease his wife's mind and make her feel secure.

After you and your partner identify your individual hand-me-down beliefs, rules, and expectations, you can begin to communicate without fear. This leads to your being able to free your conversations about money from beliefs and expectations that no longer serve you. You may retain some of your own personal beliefs about money, but you'll be in a better position to forge common ground with your partner once your silent agreements are revealed and understood. Then you can draft new agreements that serve the team.

MONEY AND WORK: IS IT MY SALARY OR IS IT ME?

Sometimes silent agreements about money develop in the workplace, often connected to salaries and other forms of compensation. This is a slightly tricky area in which to uncover silent agreements because salaries need to be discussed and negotiated within the context of your work, not on the basis of your personal financial needs. When requesting a raise, even if you're thinking it, you aren't likely to reveal truths to your boss like "With my salary, I can't even afford decent babysitters." Instead, you have to be able to recognize the value of your contribution at work and translate it into dollars and cents; meanwhile, you're the one keeping tabs on your personal wishes and needs. So even though your company may set salaries in terms of the work, you may be focused on how the salary you're earning affects your survival as well as your desire for comfort and, for some of us, even luxury.

If you're lucky enough to earn a salary that covers your personal needs as well as your wants, you may find that your silent agreements tap into issues of status, self-esteem, entitlement, or fairness. However, if your salary issues involve taking care of your basic needs, your silent agreements about the money you make may reflect unspoken feelings about struggling to make it in the world. Of course, both the millionaire executive and the poorly paid restaurant worker can be driven by silent agreements to avoid poverty at all costs. Because the groundwork for our silent agreements is usually laid early in our lives, we can all be vulnerable to silent agreements about how much money we make, whether we have a million-dollar salary or a much lower one. The possibilities for what beliefs and expectations these kinds of silent agreements reflect are endless. Take Derek, for instance.

I DESERVE MORE THAN I'M BEING PAID
Sheila and Derek

Derek was a bright twentysomething who worked for a small New York City nonprofit that created arts programs for children with serious illnesses. While he was raised by energetic, gregarious parents, Derek had grown up quiet and serious. He was kindhearted and highly creative, and it was generally understood that he was the brilliant one in his group of friends.

Derek was a hard worker, dedicated to his organization's mission. He wasn't thrilled with the entry-level salary he was offered but was promised that salaries would increase as the organization grew. He was assured that the reward he would receive for helping to improve the lives of sick children would far outweigh his salary concerns, and this argument was persuasive to him. And Derek's parents were zealous community activists in Chicago, so he grew up with the ideal of bettering the world by helping others.

After four years of working long hours to help launch the organization, Derek was frustrated and broke. He was eating noodles and living with three messy roommates in a tiny fifth-floor walk-up. His friends kept urging him to ask for a raise or to find a job with a better salary. They knew that Derek wanted to help others, but they also wanted him to enjoy his twenties without always being stressed about money.

Finally, Derek took their advice and asked his boss, Sheila, for a raise. Sheila was barely thirty herself and had a casual, informal manner. She was empathic, and most of her employees viewed her as a big sister. During their meeting, Derek described his accomplishments over the previous four years and added that he wanted to continue working at the organization but that to stay he'd need to earn a higher salary. Sheila countered that theirs was an organization for people loyal to the mission who were not focused on money. She reminded him that people had worked there longer than he had without a raise; *they* really believed in helping those less fortunate. She finished by telling Derek that she was disappointed by his request for more money and wondered if he thought he was too good for this job.

Derek blew up. He accused Sheila of having no loyalty to him or to other staff members who worked extremely hard to make the organization successful. He called her speech about his wanting a raise "manipulative crap" and stormed out of her office. Assuming that he'd just lost his job, he started packing his things, but he was surprised to hear the jangle of Sheila's bracelets as she approached his cubicle a few minutes later. Red-faced but calm, she said, "I think we've not understood each other. Can you come to my office so we can talk this out?"

WHAT IS THE SILENT AGREEMENT?

Derek had joined the organization hopeful about changing lives and was genuinely excited to be in on the ground floor of an organization that he could help build into a group with impact. Although he wasn't materialistic, he did expect to make enough money to hang out with his friends and to go to a movie now and then or on a date outside of his living room. However, his silent agreement with himself had always been this: **I don't need much money because being able to help others is its own reward.** Sheila was a silent cosigner of this agreement. And her implication that he was selfish pushed him to lash out in a very uncharacteristic way.

While Derek was growing up, his parents were dedicated activists who often overlooked their only child's needs in the interest of the cause of the moment. They would often arrive late to—or even skip—his baseball games and debates. They almost missed his high school graduation, as they rushed from an earlier event, a voter registration rally they had helped to organize. When Derek complained about his parents' absences, they dismissed his pleas as selfish. His mother would lecture him, saying that others needed their help and that she was disappointed that he didn't see how much better off he was.

Sheila's upbringing had made being part of the silent agreement relatively simple; she could afford not to make much money. Her wealthy parents thought that she was "crazy" to pursue nonprofit work, especially because she was new at fundraising. From their point of view, it would be easier if she just donated to the causes she believed in. Even so, they indulged her with a $100,000 loan to get her started, and she also had access to their wealthy friends for fundraising. Sheila was used to having her Park Avenue family shake their heads in amusement as she pursued her various dreams, but she paid her own bills and didn't have the same financial insecurities that Derek did. If she needed it, family money was just a phone call away.

Given all that was going on beneath the surface, how could Derek and Sheila come to understand the silent agreement that kept both of them locked in an unrealistic arrangement? This one was keeping Derek broke and preventing Sheila from fairly compensating her staff. Clearly it was time to lift the silence and revise the agreement.

LIFTING THE SILENCE

You may have had the same sort of encounter with a boss, or you may still be too afraid to speak up and ask for what you're worth. These types of conflicts are often born of silent agreements and can happen for many reasons. If you're someone who avoids asserting your needs, you may be vulnerable when it comes to asking to be paid what you think you're worth. This can make it hard for you to *expect* a raise. Women are often less likely to ask for raises than men, which may relate to old internalized societal messages that tell women they should be demure and selfless. And maybe you're someone who always puts others first, making it hard for you to believe that *you* deserve a raise. After all, if you're always relegating yourself to the bottom of the list (and there's always a list), you undoubtedly find it hard to focus on your own monetary needs and desires. In fact, doing such may give you a mild sense of unease, as if desire for money reflects a character flaw and proves that you're selfish. This could be what lies under a silent agreement with yourself that keeps you from asking for the raises you deserve.

Maybe you grew up with a lot of money that left you feeling slightly uncertain about being accepted for who you truly are. Maybe you never liked the focus on how much money your family has and silently vowed to yourself that you would never wear it as a badge of honor. This might lead you to behave in ways that obscure the fact that you are well off: wearing grungy clothes, hanging out in the economically disadvantaged parts of town, and choosing jobs and causes that are "down with the people" while offering minimal monetary reward. You might even find yourself overcompensating for your privileged background by staying under the money radar and avoiding any talk of money and raises, especially your own. Like Sheila, you might also react when others show interest in making and having more money for themselves.

If you find yourself in a conflict over fair compensation for the work that you do (whether the conflict is with yourself or out in the open with your boss), you may have a silent agreement. You can begin to uncover it by examining what annoys or disappoints you most about the conflict you're having. Because most disappointments embody both expectations and beliefs, if you can start with the element that is most easily identified—your disappointment—and work backward from there, you can begin the process of uncovering the silent agreement.

ASK YOURSELF

- What disappointed me about this conflict/ encounter?

- What did I expect to happen instead?

- What beliefs do I have that would lead me to expect a different exchange?

Your responses are likely to shed some light on the unspoken expectations that you and the other party brought to the conflict. And when trying to get to the bottom of this kind of conversation with a boss or supervisor, remember to adopt a tone that is congruent with your workplace. It can help to first acknowledge what your expectations were/ are and then ask how the other person sees the situation. Saying things like "I sense that you had a different idea about this" or "Maybe we're both a bit disappointed about our difficulty finding a solution so far" may open up this discussion considerably. Shedding light on your silent agreements about fair compensation, the value of your work, and the expression of these in monetary terms is the goal. Once this is clear, you'll have a better idea about how your mismatched agreements have made it difficult for the two of you to address your differences.

DEREK'S RESPONSES MIGHT LOOK LIKE THIS

- I was disappointed that I didn't get a raise.

- I expected to get the raise, not to be insulted.

- I believe that working to help others is rewarding, but I also believe that my needs are important and should be treated as such.

SHEILA'S RESPONSES MIGHT LOOK LIKE THIS

- I was disappointed that you asked for more money.

- I expected you to accept the salary you were given, taking into consideration the satisfaction of knowing that you're helping others.

- I believe that money is relatively unimportant, as it rarely makes people happy or gives them the heart to want to change the world.

GOING FORWARD

After Derek and Sheila took the time to answer these questions, they began to see that their sides of the agreement were similar but didn't include all the issues faced by the other. Derek was able to assert that his needs shouldn't be subjugated in the name of helping others. He realized that when he blew up at Sheila, he was feeling the same emotions he'd had when his parents dismissed his needs in favor of their community work. He was hurt that she accused him of being selfish when in fact he felt that doing so much work for so little pay was quite selfless. Still, he was able to apologize to Sheila for yelling when he noted that their conflict was about a raise *in the present,* not about his childhood frustration with his parents.

Sheila could also see that while they both believed in helping others, she put little emphasis on money because she had easy access to plenty of it. Also, she acknowledged that she had a bit of disdain for money as she didn't want to feel like the "phony philanthropists" she knew who gave money to get a tax break but wouldn't lift a finger to do any actual work for those in need. Seeing that their silent agreements had similar elements (the need to help others) but had different hidden clauses (and causes), Sheila and Derek were able to leave their childhood experiences out of their new, open agreement. This new agreement said that having money and helping others can exist in the same world without one obscuring or judging the need for the other. On this, they could fully agree.

In your own efforts to uncover and move beyond your silent agreements, remember that there is often a partial alignment between individuals' silent agreements that complicates them. In these cases, the silent agreements can involve a similar foundational belief (e.g., the desire to help others), but a different idea of how that belief should manifest itself in *behavior* (e.g., getting paid for it versus not getting paid for it). This type of complication makes it even more important to explore the unspoken expectations and disappointments that may lie beneath your money conflict in the workplace. If you take the time to do this exploration, you can find the parts of your individual agreements that match, making it easier to come up with a solution for those parts of your silent agreements that are not aligned.

AFTER YOU'RE GONE

Alana and Aunt Clara

Alana was the kindhearted, hardworking thirty-five-year-old niece of the Santiago family's favorite Aunt Clara. Sweetly down-to-earth, Aunt Clara was known for speaking her mind, straight with no chaser. The nieces and nephews loved spending time with her, all except for Cousin Rondo. Unlike Alana and her high-achieving siblings and cousins, Rondo could barely hold a job. He was always in some kind of jam, and if he was at Aunt Clara's house, it was because he wanted something.

Since very early childhood, Alana had been close to her aunt. She would spend hours in Aunt Clara's bedroom playing with a treasured collection of handmade dolls and looking through her aunt's fashion magazines. It was Aunt

Clara who soothed Alana when kids at school teased her during her awkward years of wearing glasses and braces. Alana had learned a lot from her aunt through the years, and she credited her aunt with her thriving self-esteem. So, it was no wonder that when Aunt Clara became ill with heart disease, Alana wanted to take care of her.

Alana moved into Aunt Clara's home, although this was an emotionally difficult time for her. She treasured the chance to spend extra time with her aunt, who told her rich stories about the family, stories of heartbreak and triumph that no one had shared with her before. Alana also learned more about Aunt Clara's strong faith—how it helped her to deal with her illness and the impending end of her life.

Two years after Alana moved in, Aunt Clara passed away. The entire family was heartbroken and looked to one another for support. Shortly after the funeral, arrangements were made to pack up Aunt Clara's home and locate her will. It was widely known that Aunt Clara was careful with her money, had made good investments, and was probably sitting on a comfortable nest egg. Still, no one was more shocked than Alana to find out that Aunt Clara died with $1.2 million in her accounts! More shocking was how she chose to divide it: Aunt Clara left the bulk of her estate to her church and the remainder to her trifling nephew, Rondo. After two years of being the most dependable person in Aunt Clara's life, Alana was left with not a penny of inheritance. But for being the family screw-up, Rondo walked away with a cool $150,000.

Alana was deeply hurt and confused. Hadn't she been the one to look after her aunt's every need? Hadn't Alana uprooted herself, put her romantic life on hold, and adjusted her work schedule so she could work from home—just so that she'd be available to meet so many of her aunt's needs? Despite Alana's very comfortable salary, she couldn't understand why her aunt left her nothing. Over time, Alana's resentment of Rondo grew, as well as her doubt about whether she'd actually been special to Aunt Clara at all.

WHAT IS THE SILENT AGREEMENT?

Alana's surprise at her aunt Clara's will is a giveaway that there was a silent agreement at work. For Alana, the revelation of the content of Aunt Clara's will negated all the talk of how special they were to each other. In her fog of upset, Alana was missing the point of the silent agreement: It had nothing to do with money or her lack of specialness. The silent agreement with her aunt went like this: **You're helping me because of our special bond and our mutual appreciation.** While Alana had signed on to this silent agreement, her reaction to the will signaled that something else was going on with her, and she needed to acknowledge it. Perhaps there was a hidden clause in Alana's silent agreement that said: **Our special bond will show up in the money left to me.** Yet how could that be? Alana had never even thought about Aunt Clara's will while she was taking care of her, nor before that. But silent agreements are like that. For years they can lie buried until one day they emerge and leave people genuinely shaken.

LIFTING THE SILENCE

Often when a family member dies, old hurts, resentments, and unresolved conflicts come to the surface and exacerbate the loss. Until Alana knew about her aunt's will, she'd been content with her role in her aunt's final months, but after the reading of the will, Alana felt unappreciated and genuinely hurt. Then she found relief after doing the following exercise, designed for helping people survive a loss. If you are in this position, answering the questions can be helpful to you, too. Try to answer in simple, specific terms.

- What did I get from this relationship?

- What did I give to this relationship?

- Which part of this relationship is over for me?

- Which part of this relationship continues for me?

- What expectations do I have for this relationship now that my loved one is gone?

- How have my expectations been challenged, and how do I feel about that?

ALANA'S RESPONSES MIGHT LOOK LIKE THIS

- I gained unconditional love, companionship, life lessons, fun, appreciation, and a sense of specialness from this relationship.

- I gave time, companionship, unconditional love, care, and appreciation to this relationship.

- The companionship, time, fun, caretaking, and sense of specialness are over for me.

- The unconditional love, appreciation for Aunt Clara, and life lessons continue for me.

- I expected to continue to feel the unconditional love, appreciation, and sense of specialness now that Aunt Clara is gone.

- When I found out that Aunt Clara left me no money, I no longer felt special or appreciated.

Each question allows you to focus on an aspect of the loss that is significant to you. When the death of a loved one is paired with expectations about money, the focus often shifts to whether we were left an inheritance. It's important to know that sometimes those financial choices aren't intended to assign degrees of significance to relationships but rather are often just expressions of silent feelings, beliefs, and expectations.

GOING FORWARD

As Alana performed this exercise, she couldn't deny how important it had become to her to feel special in her aunt's eyes. Her aunt had been a model of independent womanhood, and that had helped Alana to become confident, take chances, and forge a successful career path. There was more to it than that, though. Alana had become used to feeling that she was *more* special to her aunt than any of the other relatives were. That's why she struggled so much with her aunt's willing her estate to her flaky cousin and to a church to which her aunt hadn't seemed particularly attached. Alana's examination of the silent agreement helped her realize that she'd expected her aunt's estate to reflect the special place she'd held in Aunt Clara's heart. When she realized that she was the one who had woven money through the picture of an otherwise extraordinary relationship, she felt better and canceled her silent agreement.

You might not be waiting to see if your favorite relative left you money in her will, but you probably have your own experiences with family or friends and money and the silent agreements that often go with them. For example, your silent agreements may manifest with friends who borrow or lend you money, grown kids who won't contribute or move out of the house, or your ex-spouse, the "fun dad," spoiling the children with extravagant gifts that you can't afford. Maybe your silent agreements are at odds with your good friend's notion of what a loan is and her expectation that when you "lend" her money, you really don't want it back. And is it possible that you have a mutual silent agreement with your adult kids despite your frequent complaints about their not moving out? In this instance, you all might silently agree that as long as they stay at home and act like big kids, no one in the family (including you) has to face their fears of getting older. And that ex-spouse of yours—you might look deeper and have to admit that the two of you have been silently agreeing for years to fight a "Who's the Favorite Parent?" battle.

Whatever your silent agreements may be with yourself or others, it's these points of conflict that can often tip you off to their existence. Even if you're not openly at war, it's helpful to take note of how money flows in and out of your hands, to whom it flows, and whether there might be more to that story.

It helps to remember that when it comes to money-based silent agreements, money may be the topic, but quite often it's *not* the issue.

WHAT'S *YOUR* BOTTOM LINE?

Silent agreements about money are easily disguised as money problems and habits. If you can manage your financial life in a way that leaves you feeling secure and comfortable, you may mistakenly believe that you have no silent agreements about money. Don't be too sure. As you've already seen, what you believe about yourself, your childhood, your partners, and life in general can all have something to do with how you deal with money. It's helpful to remind yourself of your beliefs, assumptions, and expectations about money as you encounter financial challenges over the course of your life. Moments of transition and change may bring you face-to-face with financial decisions and the silent agreements underlying them. Marrying, changing careers, having children, buying a home, and retiring are just some of life's junctures where your silent agreements about money will appear. Understanding your expectations and assumptions about money can help in those critical moments where money is sure to be on your mind. Once you're aware of them, you'll be well served if you then look closer. The following questions will give you some ideas about how to do this.

My Beliefs About Money

When did I first start believing this?

What memory do I have that's connected to this belief?

How valid is this belief?

Is there another way to look at it?

My Assumptions About Money

What basis do I have for my assumptions?

How can I examine whether my assumptions are valid?

Whom can I ask? How can I test it?

If it's true, how do I feel about it?

My Expectations About Money

How realistic are my expectations?

How closely does reality match my expectations?

Why or why not?

By using these questions as guides, you'll see that whatever you're doing with your money involves a backstory.

Our formative experiences with money are spread out throughout our lives and often serve as triggers or contention. As a result, silent agreements are bound to arise in this arena and affect how we handle money and relate to others where money is involved. But we don't have to be at the mercy of our money or the silent agreements connected to it. With some effort and exploration of our silent agreements, we can emerge from old habits, beliefs, and expectations to have a healthier relationship with money and with those people who are affected by how we handle ourselves financially.

CHAPTER 5

SILENT AGREEMENTS ABOUT COMMITMENT

They broke up because John doesn't want marriage."

"Michael is the kind of guy who can't be with just one woman."

"I think Tricia won't move in with Kevin because she's commitment phobic."

Sound familiar?

Fear of commitment wears many disguises. For instance, we've all known serial monogamists. They remain romantically involved with one person for a few years but then run for the exit as soon as their partner asks for more. Then there's the short-term serial monogamist. This person's relationships usually last no more than a few weeks or months, and there's always a "good" reason why the relationship didn't continue. And of course there's also the player who doesn't pursue genuine relationships at all; he's about chasing, conquering, and getting out fast.

Relationships that involve at least one commitment avoider are usually fraught with silent agreements. But commitment avoidance certainly isn't limited to the romantic domain. Have you ever known a serial professional? This person accepts a new position, stays with it for a relatively short while, and then quits, arguing that "the boss was crazy" or "the work wasn't fulfilling." The constant job switching impedes the person's career advancement, yet he or she doesn't acknowledge a connection between the two. Another type of serial professional is the person with countless ideas for business ventures who moves from one scheme to another but falls out with his business partners just as the venture appears ready to take off. Both types of professional commitment avoidance include silent agreements.

Silent agreements are also present in the lives of professionals who stay put. The woman who sits in a cubicle for twenty years while yearning for a corner office has a different kind of commitment issue, and silent agreements help keep her stuck in that chair. She won't commit to the ambitious and assertive behavior necessary to fulfill her dreams because she's silently agreed not to ruffle any corporate feathers. In each of these scenarios, silent agreements derail people's ability to commit to a goal, a career, or another person.

There are many reasons people avoid commitment, and fear is a big one—fear of incompetence, fear of being vulnerable, fear of being exposed, and fear of personal inadequacy. We also shun commitment because of our preconceived ideas about how difficult relationships are or how much they will require of us, and because of concerns about whether someone is truly "the one." We avoid commitment because of the stories we tell ourselves about what it means to be committed. Silent agreements are usually at the heart of all of this resistance, and the good news is that people can change their patterns if they become dedicated to healthier kinds of communication and behavior. That kind of commitment requires courage, but it's the path to a much more fulfilling life.

We can illuminate the role that silent agreements play in the area of commitment by identifying three kinds of commitment:

- Commitment to an idea or way of thinking

- Commitment to a type of relationship that you want to have

- Commitment to a specific person despite challenges

The three categories often overlap; however, when you explore each one of these, you can determine where your greatest silent agreements about commitment lie.

COMMITMENT TO THE IDEA OF A RELATIONSHIP

Bob is tall, good-looking, bold, funny, and charming—a stereotypical lady magnet. His current girlfriend, Nina, a bright and positive young woman, ignores his flirting and forgives his occasional cheating by telling herself that it's a small price to pay for being with such a catch. His betrayals hurt her deeply, but she thinks that in time, he'll change. The fact that he chose her still makes her feel special, because she believes that many women would love to have him.

Bob reinforces Nina's sense of being special by telling her repeatedly that she is the "only woman who means anything" to him. He treasures her loyalty because he also has a deep need to feel special, and he tests the strength of Nina's loyalty with his endless flirtations and dalliances. Nina's occasional complaints are of little concern to him because she always forgives him. The storm always passes.

After a couple of years of this, Nina begins to doubt that this relationship can or should last. Then Bob humiliates her with another infidelity, and she decides it's time to move on. Bob believes that she's the woman who will love him no matter what, but her discontent is clear. Fearing that she might actually leave him, he surprises her with a marriage proposal. Although Nina's instincts make her hesitate, she says yes, believing that Bob's willingness to commit signals a new direction for their relationship.

Where this story leads is no surprise. For several months, they're giddy in their new life together—moving into a new home, decorating, and entertaining their friends as a married couple. Then Bob starts going out alone. At first he's just "hanging with the fellas," but then he graduates into longer nights that lead to his coming home in the early mornings with no explanations. Nina catches him in a few lies and expresses her anger and frustration. He continues to flirt in front of her when they do go out together, and she continues to complain. Pretty soon neither one feels special anymore; in fact they both end up miserable.

WHAT IS THE SILENT AGREEMENT?

The story of Bob and Nina offers a classic example of two people who are committed to the *idea* of a relationship. Bob's idea was that marriage would secure Nina's undying love for him. For Nina, marriage meant that Bob would become a faithful partner, focused only on her. The problem is that these were their assumptions *about marriage*, ideas that bore little resemblance to the truth within their actual relationship. Remember that when Bob popped the question, Nina was already contemplating leaving him. That's a pretty clear indication that even *her* sense of loyalty was wearing thin, and Bob had shown her that he was not the kind of man who would be faithful to his wife. He would be discreet, not faithful, and she knew this. These two maintained a strong commitment to the silent agreement that allowed them to get married: **They both had silently agreed that as long as they remained in the relationship, their union would make them feel special**, something they had difficulty feeling on their own.

After reading their story, you might be asking, Did Bob want to be married at all? Did he want to be a husband? Probably not. The reality was that Bob married Nina so he wouldn't lose her. He did not intend to change his behavior. He loved the rush that flirting and cheating gave him, and Nina's tolerance led him to believe that he was truly special to her. He "committed" to getting married, but he never committed to what Nina had assumed—that his "I do" meant that he'd finally become a faithful partner. On the other side of the equation, Nina wasn't planning to fulfill Bob's silent expectation that she would live within his notion of unconditional love because she *did* have conditions; one of them was that he had to stop cheating. Thus she was committed to the idea of the relationship and to a husband she *wanted*, not to the one she actually had.

LIFTING THE SILENCE

Where Do I Start? What Do I Say?

If you've ever been in a situation like this, Bob and Nina's story might help you to see that this relationship can't continue as it is. These two are trying to achieve feelings of specialness that the other party cannot provide. They need to figure out how to feel this way on their own and release the other from that responsibility. Just as is true for any of us, once they're able to appreciate their own value, their view of the relationship they have is likely to be less distorted. It might then be possible for Bob to stop flirting and cheating because he won't feel the need any longer. Although Bob has some great qualities, the relationship might be over regardless of whether he stops flirting and cheating. Nina might decide that she prefers someone more down-to-earth, less flashy, and less dependent on attention from other women. But the two certainly can't continue as they are and expect to be happy, so the existing silent agreement needs to go. It's a recipe for years of anger, distrust, and misery.

So where do you go when you're in a relationship like this one, with each of you trying to fix something that you haven't fully acknowledged? You would need to have a long and deeply honest conversation about what being married means to each of you, what your expectations are, and how you'd like your life together to unfold. In this case, Nina has to be absolutely clear that the flirting and cheating have to stop. Bob needs to be honest about whether he is willing or able to make that happen. He also needs to express what "loving him no matter what" really looks like to him, and Nina needs to decide if she can or wants to be a part of that agreement. If they can agree on a relationship that represents what they actually want and one that they can both fully commit to, they can adjust their agreement to support a healthy and sustainable relationship in which their commitment is to each other and to the new reality-based relationship they will forge.

These two are excellent candidates for couples therapy, regardless of whether they want to remain married. But even before beginning therapy, they might try to communicate on their own with some of the the classic conversation starters you have seen throughout the book:

1. I feel that . . .
2. To me, being married means . . .
3. It hurts me when . . .
4. I think I've avoided talking about this because . . .
5. I would like to . . .
6. Going forward, it's my hope that . . .

Continuing, they could try to make the statements that reflect an effort to understand the other person's feelings and thoughts:

1. I can understand why you see it that way.
2. I hear you.

3. I didn't know you felt that way.
4. I'll try to imagine what that feels like for you.
5. I get it that you . . .

They can also seek out each other's thoughts and feelings with questions like:

1. What do you think about that?
2. Does this come as a surprise to you?
3. Does this make sense to you?
4. Do you see why we can't continue as we are?
5. Is there a middle ground we can agree upon, or are you willing to agree to disagree?

GOING FORWARD

In this situation, both Nina and Bob need to try to develop a sense of their own value and specialness, separate from the relationship. This is where psychotherapy and counseling can be helpful. It is likely that silent agreements from the past are unknowingly being activated and may be getting in the way of their ability to work through this on their own. They're looking for validation from the outside, and that's a mistake. If you link your value to the opinions and actions of another person, what happens when the other person no longer supports you? What happens when she or he disappears or betrays you?

Nina and Bob were affected by the old *silent* expectations they each brought to their relationship, so going forward, they need to look very honestly at what those are and how they might be restructured to allow for a different kind of future. If they divorce, they might move on to new relationships, and for the health of those new relationships, these two need more self-awareness and understanding of any unconscious silent agreements they may be bringing into their new relationship. Also for the sake of any future unions, they must become better communicators who can start by talking to their new partners about their silent expectations. Too often, people think that talking about the grit and reality—the *terms*—of a relationship will strip away the romance. But in fact, it's the best way to know that you and your partner are entering into the same relationship, not two different fantasies of it.

It should be noted that some couples choose to remain in relationships where infidelity is the norm. Often there are cultural, religious, and/or community imperatives that lead people to this choice. When the idea of marriage includes elements that two people deem more important than fidelity—elements like status in the community or financial stability—the couple may decide to remain married despite the lack of fidelity in the relationship. Such a couple will often find a way to remain together while silently agreeing to sacrifice their personal satisfaction in favor of the ideas about marriage that they and others hold. For Nina, infidelity isn't part of the deal, and she needs to be very clear about that, either with Bob or with her next partner.

These two may look like a dramatic example of dysfunction and immaturity, but in some ways they represent the fundamentals that can underlie any marriage. Although you may say your wedding vows at the same time, often you and your spouse don't actually *get married* at the same time or in the same way. That is to say, sometimes one or the other of you may lag behind in your ability to fully commit to the marriage. Similarly, what one has in mind about the institution of marriage may not match at all what the other thinks it is. When your individual silent agreements are shaping ideas about commitment and your ideas are out of sync, you can end up feeling that you and your mate have committed to two different marriages.

COMMITMENT TO THE RELATIONSHIP—WORK LIFE

Mark and Jeremy

Sometimes the primary commitment between individuals is to the relationship itself. While you may care about and respect each other, you may also have an idea about how a particular relationship *should* be. In this type of commitment, the predominant connection is to the relationship, whether or not the relationship is ideal or even healthy. When you have this type of commitment to a relationship in the workplace, it can sometimes interfere with your ability to move forward professionally. Jeremy is a good example of this.

Just before Jeremy's freshman year in college, he worked as an intern for Mark, a business owner who would later become his boss. Mark noticed that Jeremy was mature and hardworking, so he invited Jeremy back to work for him during summers, and when Jeremy graduated, Mark offered him a job. Jeremy was grateful and worked hard to validate Mark's belief in him. Through the years,

Mark often said, "We're going to do great things together." This kind of affirmation gave Jeremy even more incentive to work hard, and it paid off as he rose in the ranks of the company. He even attended graduate school at the company's expense.

After a few years Jeremy wanted to go out on his own, perhaps start his own firm. When he hinted about this, Mark waved a dismissive hand. "No need to consider that," he said. "You're doing great here. Together, we're going to take this all the way to the top." But Jeremy had different ideas for himself, and he began to talk to some of his old grad school buddies about striking out on their own.

When Mark heard about Jeremy's plans, he told Jeremy that he was disappointed and felt betrayed. Nevertheless, he offered Jeremy more money, a new title, and the opportunity to work on the company's new subsidiaries. Jeremy was confused and didn't know what to do.

WHAT IS THE SILENT AGREEMENT?

Jeremy and Mark shared a silent agreement that they could trust each other and would always show each other professional respect and unwavering support. Mark had an extra clause in his silent agreement that expected lifelong loyalty, but it wasn't part of their shared agreement. As time passed, they became even more invested in each other. Jeremy had mixed feelings about leaving the company because Mark had been like a father to him, and he was deeply grateful for all Mark had done for him. For Mark, the relationship was equally important, and in Jeremy, he saw himself. Mark was committed to helping the young businessman make the most of his career and had long expected that Jeremy would be his successor, the one he could trust to carry his legacy forward.

LIFTING THE SILENCE

Where Do I Start? What Do I Say?
This pair's understanding of and commitment to their relationship was similar in many ways. Aspects of this agreement had worked well for years, and their mutual respect and support for each other is testament to that. However, in its current state, the relationship no longer works for both, so they need to acknowledge that more money, position, and opportunity at the company do not address the core problem with their silent agreement: Things change and it's time for Jeremy to go out on his own.

When you have a relationship that involves your work and livelihood, addressing the silent agreement is complex. Before you have a conversation to clear the air, we recommend preparing for it in the following ways:

1. Write your thoughts and feelings about both the opportunity to move on and the obstacles to such a move.
2. Discuss the situation with a trusted mentor who has your interests at heart but who also understands the issues involved in the workplace.
3. Discuss it with family members or other people who know you outside of your work life. They may understand the patterns you bring

to your relationships and may be able to help
you understand why your commitment to the
relationship is making this decision difficult.
Professional coaching can also be helpful toward
this end.

If you follow these steps, you can gain insight into the situation and shift the stories you've been telling yourselves about the relationship. Sometimes these conversations to reveal silent agreements can be transformative, but they can also become dramatic and painful if you're not prepared for candid and open conversation. So before initiating this kind of sensitive encounter with a colleague, give the person a little notice. And a rehearsal isn't a bad idea either. To help lift the silence, you might first practice on your own by using some of the following phrase starters:

1. I'm grateful for . . .
2. To me, this relationship means . . .
3. I expected . . .
4. I think I've avoided talking about this because . . .
5. Going forward, I hope that . . .

During the conversation, try to respond with sentiments that validate the other's feelings and thoughts:

1. I can understand why you see it that way.
2. I hear you.
3. I probably could have been clearer.

It also helps you to be sure that each of you is understanding the other's position when you solicit the other person's ideas and feelings with questions like:

1. What do you think about that?
2. Does this make sense to you?
3. How do you think we might be able to work this out?

GOING FORWARD

For Mark and Jeremy, there are aspects of this mutual commitment that both men value. They can build on this common ground to create a more flexible way to express and maintain their commitment. And who knows? Maybe they'll be able to partner in some other way as Jeremy pursues his own business goals. Meanwhile, Mark can enjoy the good feelings that come from knowing that he has greatly contributed to the development of the next business generation.

In your own work relationships, similar efforts can bring positive results. It is possible to remain committed in a way that works for everyone after you have recognized and talked about your silent agreements. Once unspoken expectations and assumptions are out in the open in your work relationships, there is a clearer path to understanding what this commitment needs to look like for both of you to thrive in it.

COMMITMENT TO THE
RELATIONSHIP—LOVE LIFE

Geneva and Lance

Sometimes a couple's commitment to their relationship is based on a very clear awareness of what the relationship is rather than what they might fantasize that it is or could be. Whether or not their interaction is healthy isn't the core issue here, as is illustrated by some relatively unhappy couples who stay together "for the children." People often choose to remain in a relationship despite personal discontent because the union provides something important to them. Maybe they're motivated by financial security, an unwillingness to disrupt the routines of their children, or an aversion to the idea of divorce. In other cases, the commitment is to a relationship that is fulfilling for both people. Happy relationship or not, healthy dynamics or not, couples committed specifically to the relationship may have silent agreements fortifying the union.

Geneva and Lance's healthy silent agreement supports their commitment, despite the fact that they both view their relationship as only temporary. They're Midwesterners who fell in love during their senior year in college and moved into a New York apartment shortly after graduation. For two years, they enjoyed the romance and thrills of being a young couple in the big city. Then came the inevitable questions about their future. Geneva's family didn't approve of Geneva's new city ways and wondered when she was going to get serious about settling down to a more traditional life. Lance's family—full of religious married couples—denounced his failure to "make an honest woman of her."

What their families didn't know was that Lance and Geneva didn't intend to marry each other. Lance loved Geneva but planned to pursue a career that would involve extensive travel. He didn't want to begin a marriage under the strain of that kind of distance. He also wasn't interested in remaining celibate while away on lengthy assignments. Geneva had her own reasons for not wanting the relationship to lead to a marriage. While growing up, she had watched women in her family struggle to sustain long-distance relationships, and she didn't want that kind of frustration in her own life. And although she loved Lance, given his aversion to being celibate while away from her, she couldn't see herself being with him long term.

WHAT IS THE SILENT AGREEMENT?

Geneva and Lance had each silently agreed to remain in the relationship while they adjusted to living in New York and to use it as an anchor as they transitioned into life after college. The agreement was working well. They enjoyed each other and the security of having someone to lean on as they navigated an unfamiliar city and the challenges of moving from college life to independent adulthood. As time went on, and thanks to the curiosity and concern of their families, Lance and Geneva began to feel that they should discuss whether they each envisioned a future that included the other.

LIFTING THE SILENCE

For Geneva and Lance, lifting the silence was relatively easy. Although they never allowed the "meddling" of their families to push them in unwanted directions, in time it became clear to the couple that they should begin to talk about the future. They were fortunate that their silent agreements aligned so well. More often than not, at least one person in a long-term relationship wants the union to continue indefinitely, so the discovery that the other person isn't planning to work toward forever can come as a painful jolt. Sometimes, though, you might get together at a time in your life when the relationship is fun and easy but never really has the flavor of something you want to continue forever. Geneva and Lance candidly acknowledged that although theirs was a good relationship, they didn't want it to become a marriage. With a clear understanding that sooner or later they would part, they felt happy to enjoy the present and to help each other with their respective futures. And they made clear to their families that they didn't want to hear any more questions about their plans.

GOING FORWARD

Ending the silence of their agreement allowed Lance and Geneva to remain close and loving toward each other as they transitioned to the next phase of their lives. When it was time to part ways romantically, their relationship evolved into a loving friendship. Had they wanted to try to stay together, they could have discussed strategies to manage the challenges of long distance and have considered whether Geneva would be willing to travel with Lance whenever possible. They might have also considered whether Lance could try to limit the frequency of his trips. But given that they were both comfortable with eventually going in different directions, they were able to continue as supportive partners in the relationship with a full understanding of where it was going and where it was not.

You may have experienced a similar relationship scenario, one in which you've both accurately discerned the nature of your relationship despite not having openly discussed it. At some point when you're ready to part, you're likely to have a less dramatic and difficult conversation than if your agreements didn't align. The fact that they do align is a lucky coincidence in these situations, but most of us can't count on this when we've spent a long time with someone. If you can check in with your partner along the way to make sure that your agreements do line up, you can part as friends and carry sweet memories of the relationship as you move on.

COMMITMENT TO A PERSON

Dan and Christine

The final category of commitment that people often engage in is absolute commitment to a person. Silent agreements sometimes accompany this commitment, and such agreements are often related to what the other person represents for you. For instance, this kind of silent agreement might be based in a promise to yourself that you'll choose a certain kind of partner to avoid the types of difficult re-lationships that you witnessed while growing up. Or your silent agreement might keep you in a relationship that you know is highly dysfunctional because you're trying to re-pair a past unhealthy relationship by making the current one work. You may be clear that you don't enjoy the person or the relationship—you might even be miserable in it—but you feel a need to stay because your partner represents a chance to heal. In cases like these, if the commitment is to the person more than to the relationship itself, the effort to unearth the silent agreement can often be challenging.

Sometimes one person's commitment to another per-son can be very confusing to people outside the relation-ship but easily understood by those *in* the relationship. These relationships might find you saying, "They are the most unlikely couple," or "I don't get what he sees in her." The story of Christine and Dan offers a clear example of this kind of silent agreement.

Christine and Dan, both native New Yorkers, met while in college. They're good-looking, social, and fun-loving and were instantly attracted to each other. Soon they declared their relationship exclusive, and together they spent a lot of time at parties and in bars being very social with their big circle of friends. Now and then Dan's buddies would tell him that they'd seen Christine appearing to be a little too friendly with one or another of the many guys who approached her. Over the next four years, rumors swirled about her involvement with this fellow or that one, but Dan ignored them and continued to affirm his love for her.

One day three of Dan's buddies sat him down for an intervention of sorts, adamant about their suspicions that his girl was hooking up with other guys. Dan brushed it off: "Look, I knew she was a flirt when I met her. Hell, that's how we got together! Anyway, I love her and I want her to have fun. There's no evidence that she's messing around. We're fine." His friends didn't bring it up after that, but away from Dan, they agreed that he was in massive denial and was headed for heartache.

Christine continued her flirtatious ways, but she was always lively, sensuous, and attentive whenever she and Dan were together. To the surprise of Dan's friends, Dan proposed, and a few months later he and Christine married. At the wedding, Dan's friends whispered their doubts to one another, fueled by the fact that some of her rumored hookups were at the wedding!

A few years later, Dan and Christine had two children and were settled into a new home. They went on to build a solid and long relationship that continued to grow. Whenever they would get together with their old gang, their friends would remark that the two seemed very compatible and extremely happy.

WHAT IS THE SILENT AGREEMENT?

On the surface, it might seem to you that Dan was deluding himself by remaining with someone who was not able to be faithful to him. His friends tried to warn him that Christine wasn't good for him; they didn't trust her. What they didn't know was that **for Dan, the relationship was defined by his commitment to Christine. Period.** He could tolerate her flirtations and possible hookups because he saw them as a reflection of aspects of her personality that he found highly attractive. She was somewhat outrageous, spontaneous, lusty, and fun, and he loved all that about her. **He simply wanted *her* and silently agreed to accept the rest of it.** Christine also had a part in this agreement; **her side of it said that if Dan allowed her to be herself without judgment or a demand that she change her flirtatious ways, her love would be shared with him alone. They both silently agreed that they would be faithful in their love for each other and understood that when Christine was done flitting around, their commitment to each other would remain, steady and strong.**

LIFTING THE SILENCE

Should We?

When your silent agreement is working, there isn't a compelling reason to change or eliminate the agreement; if your nontraditional arrangement makes other people uncomfortable, that isn't your problem. But there's often value in lifting the silence. When you are both clear about your desired parameters and about what you feel is acceptable, that openness can prevent misunderstandings and hurt feelings. Dan and Christine went a long time without discussing these aspects of their relationship, and while their relationship remained intact and mutually satisfying, being open about the terms of the relationship wouldn't have been a bad idea.

Some might think that Christine and Dan have a lopsided agreement. By not demanding faithfulness from

Christine, is Dan revealing that he doesn't value himself? That might have been the case if Dan had had a commitment to a particular type of relationship, but what mattered most to Dan was his commitment to *Christine*. Although Christine may not have been fully monogamous during their pre-marriage years, she agreed in her own way to remain committed to Dan; she agreed that he was the most important one and that in time she would be all his in every way.

This might not be a popular idea of a healthy silent agreement, but it worked for this couple because their commitments matched. As a result, they were able to have an agreement based on who they truly were, driven primarily by their desire to be with each other.

GOING FORWARD

The agreement between Dan and Christine has given them a strong foundation. Over time they might decide to reconstruct the agreement if it needs adjusting due to individual or life changes. Theirs is a relationship based on a mutual commitment to the other person specifically, and that kind of commitment can fortify a relationship very effectively. Because above all it is Dan whom Christine wants most and Christine whom Dan values most, the two will likely remain solid.

This kind of relationship is often the subject of love songs and literature. That's because this type of undying commitment to another person suggests a steadfastness and sense of security that many hope for in their intimate relationships.

COMMITMENT TO OURSELVES

When you have a commitment with yourself that you silently agree to uphold, you're hitting all three levels of commitment at once: a commitment to a person (yourself), to a relationship (with yourself), and to an idea (of yourself). These types of silent agreements can serve as powerful guides for how we move through the world. All of us probably have dozens of silent agreements that help us to determine whom we connect with in our lives, how we behave at home and at work, and how we view ourselves or the selves we strive to be. "I will never lie to my children." "I will always be there for my friends." "I will never date a small-minded person." "I will always stand up for myself." These kinds of silent agreements are positive and helpful. Who can argue with being committed to honesty, loyalty, good relationship judgment, and self-confidence?

On the other hand, we can also walk with commitments to ourselves that involve negative silent agreements. "I am always the victim." "I'll never make enough money." "I need to learn to be satisfied with what I have." "I will stick with him/her because it's better than being alone." When we commit to these kinds of notions of ourselves and act them out in our lives, we may line up our behavior to bring our silent agreements to life. Our commitment to a negative or limited idea of ourselves can derail relationships, short-circuit our possibilities, and cause us self-inflicted pain.

To avoid this, we need to check in with ourselves to explore which silent agreements we have committed to and determine how they're showing up in our lives. You have likely silently agreed to commit to a notion of yourself, others, or life in general if you're telling yourself:

- I never . . .

- I always . . .

- I can't see myself doing . . .

- No matter what, I end up . . .

- Things never change for me.

- I can't seem to stop . . .

Once you examine the ways in which your commitment to your silent agreements is affecting your life, you'll be in a better position to make changes if needed, to discard old commitments that no longer fit, or to keep the ones that are working for you. This process is not unlike those we have outlined throughout the book. Being candid with yourself about what has led you to these commitments in the first place is essential. Exploring old messages from your childhood can help you to do this while you note:

- what you fear

- what you are trying to control

- what pain you want to avoid

- how you see yourself

- how you want to see yourself

Through this process, you can help yourself to make better choices about the silent agreements you commit to, facilitating positive outcomes in your life.

All silent agreements are rooted in past experiences and in the expectations that we bring to our relationships. The silent agreements that underscore a commitment to a relationship, a person, or an idea of how a relationship should function often serve to solidify those commitments, even though they may confuse people on the outside who don't understand the specific arrangement. Whether a commitment-based silent agreement governs our notions of acceptable behaviors, limits, or other relationship "rules," communication will always help to prevent the kinds of potentially painful misunderstandings that can erupt when silent agreements aren't compatible.

CHAPTER 6

SILENT AGREEMENTS ABOUT FAMILY

As long as there are families, there will be silent agreements between siblings, between cousins, between parents and children, between children and their grandparents, and on and on from weddings to reunions to anniversaries to funerals. Sometimes these silent agreements are even passed down through generations. Some of the richest soil for silent agreements exists in the realm of parenting. The pressure to reproduce is ever present, even for committed couples who have decided to be child-free. And of course there are countless issues and expectations that arise for couples who do choose to raise children. Because family dynamics can be so complex and run so deeply, silent agreements often develop and thrive within familial relationships.

Many of us have lived with family dysfunction. Separation and divorce—which often include custody arrangements and financial agreements, as well as emotional issues—have affected millions of people, whether or not they or their parents were the ones divorcing. While there are countless guidebooks to help with the issues of divorce, there are no rulebooks, so as people try to work through the tricky process of blending families, there will be bumps in the road. These bumps are the results of many factors, including dealing with loss and the stigma of divorce, and expanding the family to include stepparents, stepsiblings, and half-siblings. The blending of families can often pave the way for silent agreements.

PARENTING IN A BLENDED FAMILY

Bill and Denise

Denise, thirty-seven, was a volunteer at a local mission that helped to feed and house homeless veterans, and Bill, forty-six, was one of the organization's largest donors. Volunteering helped Denise cope with the stress of being the single parent of two young boys whose father had been absent for years. It also added meaning to a life made tedious by an unchallenging paralegal job and an almost nonexistent social life. Bill, having been raised in a military family, felt an affinity for veterans and was dedicated to helping them. The two met at the mission's annual fundraiser the night that Bill was the keynote speaker. Later that evening, Bill invited Denise to meet at a restaurant to discuss how the two of them might work together to further the mission's goals. They felt instant chemistry and opted to spend more time together, which was no small task for Denise because she was running out of friends who could watch her sons, Gabriel and Shane.

Denise and Bill began to see each other regularly, and Denise was attracted to Bill's steadiness and his structured life, which she imagined would be an asset to her and her sons in the wake of the boys' father's drug-fueled abandonment of the family. After all, Bill had been married and had raised two daughters who were living successful lives as responsible adults.

Bill was initially attracted to Denise for her relaxed and fun-loving style. She was spontaneous and brought laughter into his life. They appeared very happy as they went on long walks, attended church together, and dined at fine restaurants. They both enjoyed no longer feeling lonely, and Denise was especially relieved that Bill seemed to like the boys and that they looked forward to seeing him.

During Bill's childhood, when kids were told to make their beds, they sprinted to their rooms and pulled the sheet corners tight in anticipation of the quarter-bounce test. When they heard "Dinner is ready!" they dropped everything to take their places in their designated seats at the table, where they never spoke with food in their mouths. In his adolescence, Bill sometimes slept the night on the front porch knowing that because he'd come home after curfew, his father wouldn't let him in the house. When Bill became a parent, *D* stood for *discipline* first and *devotion* second—devotion to God, country, and family, in that order.

Denise was raised very differently. In her childhood home, everyone was given the right to speak and express opinions. Punishments were always gentle—often no more than a serious conversation to help the kids understand the impact of their actions. As a parent, Denise became a similar kind of disciplinarian. She would issue time-outs to her children and encourage them to think about their behavior and consider what they might do differently next time.

Bill and Denise had a yearlong courtship filled with fun and togetherness. They loved bowling, going to movies, and taking road trips to theme parks with the boys playing happily in the back seat. Shane and Gabriel were beginning to love the idea of being in a family again, although they secretly wondered if their father was still alive and whether they would ever see him again.

One year after they met, Bill and Denise got married at the mission hall; both said they'd never been happier. They were officially becoming a family. Their four children attended the wedding with joy, and Bill's daughters even stayed with the boys when Bill and Denise honeymooned in Hawaii. After the wedding, things began to change. Denise and the boys moved into Bill's three-bedroom house, and within only a few weeks Bill began complaining that his once orderly house was unkempt—shoes strewn through the halls and rooms, messy bedrooms, dirty dishes left in the sink. Bill soon realized that the differences between some of his values and preferences and those of his new wife had launched them into a recurring loop of "good cop/bad cop." Meanwhile, Denise's sons defied their stepfather's attempts to enforce discipline by avoiding him as much as possible. As the family tension increased, Denise became sadder and more insecure, and her insecurities brought back memories of her first husband's complaints: he'd blamed her for the boys' bad behavior and said that her parental incompetence was the reason he was rarely home. When Bill became more and more stern with her sons, Denise began to question other aspects of their relationship. Had it been a bad idea to try to blend her kids into a new family? Had she committed too much too soon?

Then came the call from her son's guidance counselor. Denise's hands shook as she heard that her son had reported being slapped hard on the back by his new stepfather "for not cleaning his room." The counselor said, "A social worker will be investigating this matter."

WHAT IS THE SILENT AGREEMENT?

Bill believed that strict discipline is what paves the road from child to responsible adult. He also believed that setting strict and clear boundaries is a way to express love. In his relationships, Bill had always been the one in charge, and he excelled in a leadership role. Denise believed that cultivating independence is the best way to help a child develop a solid sense of self. In her view, punishment stunts that growth and can even damage a child's well-being. The two hadn't communicated their views on parenting, and given their disparate parenting styles, they invariably ended up in conflict. **Each silently assumed that they'd be free to parent as they saw fit and that the other would parent similarly.** Bill thought that his influence would be healthy for boys whose father had disappeared into a life of addiction. Denise assumed that as the boys' natural parent, she would be the one in charge of discipline and that Bill would understand a stepparent's role, which she saw as "assistant parent." These disparities were causing daily conflict between them, so the marriage began to unravel.

LIFTING THE SILENCE

Bill and Denise were full of resentment, but both were committed to saving the marriage. When the situation became so dire that they were facing an accusation of child abuse, they committed to family therapy, where they could work toward learning to parent in a blended family. In this manner, they hoped to revive their marriage.

The way people choose to parent is influenced by many factors, beginning with their own childhoods. First, Bill and Denise could examine their own childhoods and take an honest look at how they now perceived the fairness and effectiveness of the way each was raised. Bill and Denise's silent agreement wasn't identified nor adequately addressed because their beliefs about parenting were nested in their own upbringing. Every time Bill and Denise tried to have a conversation about child-rearing, it devolved into a subtle attack on the other's parents. Bill stood behind the idea that despite his upbringing, which included strict rules, yelling, and "whoopings," he had "turned out all right." Because Denise grew up with an open-minded, lenient style of parenting, she viewed the "Bill Way" as both currently hurtful and potentially harmful in the long run.

The couple would also benefit from examining their previous relationships and assessing how their parenting styles affected the children involved. Perhaps Denise needed to consider whether to integrate some of Bill's parenting style so that the boys could learn how to respect healthy boundaries. Considering that the original role model for the boys had been an addict who abandoned them, a stable male figure could be a very healthy addition to their lives. Bill could ponder whether it's reasonable or healthy for parental discipline to be viewed as "one size fits all." Was it appropriate to parent Denise's boys using exactly the same methods he'd used with his daughters?

GOING FORWARD

Believing that therapy offered the best chance to save their marriage and build a happy family life, Bill and Denise scheduled a family therapy session for the four of them. In order for the therapy to be successful, the two will need to listen carefully to the boys and to each other. These sessions will likely be emotional and painful, but if they all commit to trying to understand one another and adapt, there's much reason to hope for success. Bill may feel defensive and frustrated, and he may resent the fact that while he's not allowed an equal voice in parenting, he still has to live with the repercussions of a completely different disciplinary style from the kind he believes in. He also needs to learn how to regain the trust of his stepsons. Denise must let go of the guilt she harbors about her boys' being abandoned by their father and must be honest with herself about how that loss led her to become too lenient in her parenting. She needs to learn to be an effective disciplinarian and not fear her sons' anger when she makes unpopular decisions. In short, both Denise and Bill need to lean toward the middle so they can hear each other better and present a loving, fair, unified parenting front.

If you find yourself in a blended family situation like Bill and Denise's, you might ask yourself the following questions to help you begin to understand the situation.

Self-Help Session

Be specific with your answers; give examples.

- How much am I willing to revise my view of a mother's and a father's role?

- Am I willing to change how I discipline my children or stepchildren?

- What does giving up control look like? How is it going to affect me?

FOR THE STEPPARENT

- What is it going to take for me to let go of control as a stepparent and let the parent be in charge?

FOR THE PARENT

- How can I maintain control of the discipline and still let the stepparent have a voice?

Blended families can be *very* happy units. If you're part of one now or preparing to become so, do your best to examine your possible silent agreements as soon as possible. This will give your family the best chance for open communication and overall success.

NONTRADITIONAL ROLES, UPSET EXPECTATIONS

Miguel and Melissa

Miguel and Melissa were lawyers in their late thirties who delayed getting married until their careers felt solid. They proved to be excellent partners as they helped each other through graduation and the establishment of their careers, staying committed to their relationship, which was the best combination of friendship and love that either had ever known. Two years after their wedding, Melissa gave birth to a girl, and fifteen months later, to a boy. With two small children in the house and demanding careers, Miguel and Melissa had much to do and took it on with vigor.

Miguel was passionate about social justice and housing rights. While his work as assistant director of a community-based organization was quite important to their inner-city community, his salary didn't reflect his effort and ability. But both Melissa and Miguel were proud of his achievements and dedication, and they shared an understanding that Miguel's passion for his work was more important than the money he brought home.

Melissa, on the other hand, had recently been promoted to the position of chief counsel in a prestigious finance company, and she planned next to become a vice president. Miguel was thrilled about Melissa's promotion despite the fact that she kept late hours and was expected to travel. Since the births of their children, Melissa had managed to function like a superwoman both at home and at work, but the stress of so many demands was beginning to show. Early in their relationship, they had vowed never to hire domestic help, and Miguel did his best to help with the at-home responsibilities. Melissa's mother had been a domestic worker who suffered terribly over not being available to her own children, and Melissa and Miguel preferred to rely on family to help with the children. In return, they shared their beautiful, spacious brownstone, which became the center of their close-knit family's gatherings.

Soon it became apparent that Miguel's efforts with the children and around the house weren't up to Melissa's standards. She complained that he mixed colors when he did the laundry, often left dishes in the kitchen sink, and was generally disorganized in dealing with bath- and bedtime. After several months of Melissa's complaints, Miguel told her with exasperation, "I give up. You do it all!" Melissa got in a few digs about the burdens of trying to be a supermom but soon realized that it was time to address what was really going on between them.

WHAT ARE THE SILENT AGREEMENTS?

When Melissa asked Miguel if he really meant it when he said, "You do it all!" Miguel sheepishly admitted that he had secretly wished she would. Despite his knowing that it wasn't fair, he'd always imagined that his wife would manage the traditional domestic tasks. **He had silently agreed to help Melissa with the child-rearing and household chores with the assumption that his help would be ancillary because she would be in charge of the domestic aspects of their lives.** Melissa was responsible for her own side of this silent agreement. She admitted that **she wanted Miguel's help because it was all just too much to do alone, but she always assumed that she would be the one in control, especially in the parenting department. So, while they both silently agreed that Melissa would be in charge of everything, Melissa had not signed on to *do* everything.**

LIFTING THE SILENCE

While the conversation was not easy, both Miguel and Melissa had to confront their disappointment and mismatched expectations as well as find the courage to be direct and vulnerable in their communication. Melissa had to come to terms with what it meant to her to be the primary provider for the family, and she was proud of herself for being able to make this significant contribution. One evening her son validated her hard work: In a parent-teacher conference at his preschool, the teachers mentioned that during snack time when the children were talking about "what their mothers made," most of them spoke of cupcakes and cookies. But Manuel boasted, "My mommy makes money!" Melissa and Miguel laughed all the way home.

Miguel began to develop pride in the fact that he was taking care of his family as a nurturer and planner. As the only male child in his traditional Puerto Rican family and the only one among his friends to share domestic tasks with his partner, Miguel had to redefine himself as a modern kind of father. Melissa revealed that she'd been very lonely as the child of a woman who was busy taking care of other people's children. This admission gave Melissa the freedom to admit that her mother's lack of control over her own life gave Melissa a strong need to be in control—of just about every aspect of her life. Miguel's new insight about his wife helped him to be more understanding of her sometimes overbearing behavior as a mother. And Melissa developed new respect for Miguel's efforts to help her. She could now see that he was struggling with his desire for a superwife while still trying to be a fully contributing husband and father. Miguel had to adjust to the fact that Melissa was bringing home significantly more income than he was and that his domestic help was key to their having a balanced family life. They began to work on a new agreement that redefined their parenting roles.

GOING FORWARD

Eventually they were able to divide their parenting tasks along lines that were practical and enjoyable for both. Even the children would eventually be expected to plan for special family days. Melissa loved to plan vacations, while Miguel enjoyed being in charge of sports activities. When Melissa had to travel, she stayed more involved with the kids, using technology for daily encounters and bedtime stories, but she avoided giving Miguel parenting directions to follow in her absence. With a new and clear understanding of their roles and the value of their contributions, they started enjoying more family time.

This couple's scenario offers an excellent example of how partners become co-owners of each other's silent agreements. It usually takes two. When Melissa spoke up about the trouble that this silent agreement was creating, she lifted the silence for which they were both responsible. Individually and together, you can hold the agreement up to the light and decide which aspects of it, if any, you want to keep and which you'd rather adjust or discard.

Self-Help

If you think that you and your partner are experiencing a silent agreement based on parenting, consider these questions to help your exploration.

- Are you willing to change your patterns to help the balance of household responsibilities?

- How much are you willing to examine and shift your preexisting ideas about the roles of a mother and a father?

- Can you visualize what a better parenting model would look like for the two of you?

- What will be different? How will each of you contribute to this new model?

I'M THE BETTER PARENT

When Alexandra was twenty, she married Lee, a man ten years her senior. Alexandra was always smiling, appearing carefree and sophisticated. She'd been born into poverty in war-torn Croatia, but she worked to rise above that hardship by taking school seriously, excelling in both academics and the arts, and working hard to develop her exceptional singing talent. She participated in regional choral competitions, and her school won an international choral competition, largely thanks to Alexandra's masterful execution of two solos. Soon afterward, a representative from an Italian cruise ship company approached her to sing on its intercontinental excursions. Alexandra left for Italy the day after graduation and never looked back.

Lee's timing was good. After earning an MBA at a prestigious American university, he proved to be a shining star in the venture capital firm he founded. He had promised to take his parents on a cruise for their thirtieth wedding anniversary, and during that getaway, he met Alexandra in one of the ship's lounges. He was mesmerized by her voice, beauty, and grace, and immediately after her set, he walked up to the stage and introduced himself. In that moment, their thrilling courtship began. Alexandra delighted in being romanced by a real-life Prince Charming. He was handsome, elegant, and cultured, and it was clear to Alexandra that he was a man—nothing like the boys who flirted and flitted around the ship. And she found his closeness to his parents irresistible. Being quickly enveloped by Lee's tight-knit family helped fill the hole that the war had torn in her heart.

Their short courtship led to a beautiful wedding, followed by a honeymoon on the Italian Riviera. Next they moved to a luxurious apartment near Wall Street and hosted elegant parties during which their guests looked out onto a gorgeous view of the Statue of Liberty. Their life together was glamorous and the envy of Alexandra's city friends, with whom she would shop and dine at the poshest stores and cafés. In the second and third years of their marriage, Alexandra gave birth to two children, a girl and then a boy. Then the stock market crash changed their financial lives; the days of lavish parties and unfettered shopping were over, and the marriage unraveled. Nine years after marrying, they divorced, and Alexandra's life became dominated by managing her children's schoolwork, the housework, the shopping, and a budget that never stretched far enough. In all her girlish dreams, she had never once imagined being a single parent.

Before the marriage ended, Alexandra's role had been to look beautiful, keep the relationship exciting, and plan their social activities. She had never paid a bill nor familiarized herself with their investment portfolio. Lee generally handled everything from paying the bills to financing elaborate vacation properties to managing all their business ventures. Above all, Lee was the provider, and that made him secretly feel secure and in charge of his world. Alexandra was the opposite: she knew how to enjoy her life by socializing, entertaining, and traveling with the others of Lee's social standing. She reveled in being the center of attention and understood the value that her charm and worldliness added to her husband's social and business life. But as the years passed, Alexandra was secretly disappointed that she and Lee no longer shared the fun and romance of their early days.

Longing for a time when her relationship had been exciting, Alexandra looked for ways to entertain herself. At first shopping filled the void, then a dalliance with gambling, then a risky affair with one of Lee's friends. Still, she felt empty. Lee thought Alexandra to be irresponsible and self-centered, while Alexandra saw Lee as critical, judgmental, and bad-tempered. They often put each other down in front of the children, and each was convinced that the other was the inferior parent. Eventually they began divorce proceedings and the battle for custody began. But the feud didn't end after they divorced, even though their constant bickering and belittling of the other was scarring their children.

WHAT IS THE SILENT AGREEMENT?

When the relationship began to deteriorate, Lee no longer seemed like a chivalrous knight, and Alexandra no longer appeared to be the delightful belle of the ball, ever appreciative of having been swept away by her charming prince. They used to share **a silent agreement that Lee was the great protector and the responsible one**, but now they are divorced, and Alexandra has taken on more responsibility as the custodial parent, so that silent agreement doesn't hold anymore.

During the custody battle, Lee was unable to view Alexandra as a good mother who could care for and protect the children in the way that he had. And Alexandra viewed Lee as a sore loser who had become negative and overly critical. Lee criticized Alexandra for overindulging the children, while she saw him as a pesky micromanager. Each came to believe himself or herself the better parent, and their bitter, resentful behavior began to diminish their children's happiness.

LIFTING THE SILENCE AND GOING FORWARD

Silent agreements that feed our own egotistic need to be the "better parent" almost always backfire. Children's love for their parents is not usually based on some kind of performance tally but rather on the parents' ability to show unconditional love. And most children eventually become aware of the strengths and weaknesses of their parents but love them in spite of their deficits. As long as Lee and Alexandra remained mired in their fantasy roles for themselves, their whole family would suffer.

The custody battle had been costly, and when it was over, little had been won. The children looked tense and miserable much of the time, and this deeply concerned relatives and friends close to the battle. It was during this time that the grandparents shared their concern about the constant quarreling between Alexandra and Lee and its effect on the children. Thanks to her focus on a new career, Alexandra was beginning to feel better about her life, so she opened up and agreed to meet with her in-laws and Lee to discuss their concerns. She accepted that their goal should be to become co-parents focused on the children's happiness. Sometimes relationships shift when one person shifts, and Lee realized it was important for them to work together for the children's sake. Lee and Alexandra even agreed to have their children receive support from a favorite school counselor.

Alexandra's long-standing agreement with herself needed to be revised to acknowledge that she would never again think like a damsel in distress. She discovered that her neediness and early trauma had contributed to her viewing herself as a girl in need of a man to rescue her. But her newfound independence and self-esteem allowed her to be a very different kind of parent, one who could listen to Lee and accept that he offered valuable ideas and even wisdom.

Lee had to come to terms with the fact that he wasn't a superhero whose worth was determined by the treasure he could win, the amount of money he could make, and the woman he could rescue. The vulnerability he felt after losing his marriage was humbling and caused him to look seriously at his life, specifically at the way he was behaving throughout the divorce. Ultimately, he realized that what matters most is that he is a loving human being who does the best he can for his children.

SELF-HELP

The following kinds of questions will be helpful to parents going through divorce who are revising silent agreements and are committed to creating the most positive scenario possible going forward:

- What am I afraid will happen if my children have a positive relationship with my ex, the person who so terribly hurt and disappointed me?

- To what degree am I willing to change what I say about the other parent for the sake of my children's well-being?

- In what ways am I willing to change how I relate to my ex-partner and take the necessary steps to co-parent more effectively?

- Will I ever be able to let go of my bitterness and resentment toward my former partner? What will that require?

- Am I finding support resources to help me find balance as a single parent?

Questions for the divorcing couple:

- Can we each find the courage to acknowledge our own responsibility in the demise of the marriage and tell our children that *both* of us played a part?

- Can we have positive conversations in the presence of the children?

- Can we commit to saying only positive or neutral things about each other in the presence of our children?

- Are we as co-parents both able to support our children by attending their events and activities and by being kind to each other at those events?

- Is it possible for us to put the negative energy of our past behind and find contentment as we build the best possible lives for these wonderful children who are products of our union?

If you're wrestling with silent agreements relative to parenting, here's some good news: While silent agreements about child-raising can be some of the most complicated to resolve, when we act in the best interests of our children instead of ourselves, we can find ourselves more dedicated to resolution. In other words, you might find that when the situation involves a minor whose care you're responsible for—a child you love—you must choose to act as your best self.

THE SINGLE CAREGIVER

Katherine

Katherine was a single, successful corporate executive in her mid-forties and was respected by her business associates, family, and friends. She'd had several long-term relationships but for various reasons had never married. When people would refer to her as "childless," she'd correct them with a smile, "Actually, I'm child-free." While her family was aware that Katherine had a good job and was financially comfortable, they knew relatively few specifics about her professional successes. Katherine's humble style made it easy for relatives to view her as "just one of us."

Despite having two able-bodied brothers, Katherine was always the one to take care of her parents. She was also often involved in the lives of her other relatives, generously helping them with advice, loans, and contributions to the college funds of several nephews and nieces. She was the fun auntie who hosted the big family reunion every year without asking for any contribution from others. And she almost never missed a family wedding, graduation, or funeral. As Katherine's parents entered their eighties, their declining health became a concern for Katherine and her two brothers, both of whom lived in other parts of the country. While her brothers visited their parents from time to time, Katherine had always been the one to spend a lot of time with their mother and father, making sure that they had everything they needed.

One day the president of Katherine's company invited her to dinner and offered her a promotion. She'd been chosen to head the company branch in London, and Katherine was elated. To make the scenario even more thrilling, she was in a growing relationship with a love interest who lived in London. As she pondered the logistics of the move, Katherine was acutely aware that in addition to her being dedicated to her extended family, she had also been the primary caregiver to her aging parents and the one most involved in solving their challenges.

At a family reunion, Katherine announced she would soon be moving to London but would return often for visits. She was jolted by her family's reactions, which included comments like "Why didn't you talk to us first?" and even "Isn't that kind of selfish?" After everything she'd sacrificed and postponed for these people, *this* was the response she received to her very happy personal news? She was so angry that she stormed out of the reunion, leaving them for hours to their own devices.

WHAT IS THE SILENT AGREEMENT?

The agreement was that **the dutiful daughter would take care of the parents forever.** After all, Katherine was the one who had created that expectation by consistently taking care of her parents and, to some degree, even of her younger brothers and their children. She loved what these close connections meant to her, but she had never examined the imbalance of it all. Through the years, Katherine had had long-term boyfriends, some of whom she'd been very serious about, but her family never asked much about these relationships. They had always expected that Katherine preferred being single and would leave it that way, and she never offered them any reason to think differently. Katherine maintained the silent agreement that **she had no significant personal life beyond her extended family, and her relatives actively participated by not asking questions.** They viewed her as always available and relatively lacking in needs. Now that she was poised to start a new chapter that assigned her focus primarily on herself, the silent agreement was going to rear its ugly head.

LIFTING THE SILENCE

After hearing her family's negative reactions to her news, Katherine began to see things in a new light. She had always put the needs of her extended family first, and she had enjoyed cultivating a selfless image in their eyes. As far as her relatives were concerned, her efforts hadn't involved sacrifice; they had simply been the actions of a dedicated daughter, sister, and aunt who preferred to focus on the lives of others than on her own. Initially this realization angered Katherine and made her relatives appear self-centered, insensitive, and even selfish. But then she examined her role in the dynamic. She had appeared to be very happy with her role as primary caregiver, so why wouldn't they have assumed that the role was one she would have been happy to play indefinitely? The fact that they didn't accept the news of her impending departure gracefully was understandable; they would simply have to adjust. She was soothed by her own acknowledgment of the idea that she was comfortable with no longer being viewed as a star in the family. For Katherine, the courage to move full speed ahead with her new plans was easy to summon because she knew that she was doing the right thing for herself. The plans included her remaining involved in the lives of those she loved, but now she'd be putting herself first.

GOING FORWARD

Katherine negotiated a mutually satisfactory arrangement that handed the primary responsibility for their parents' care to her brothers. She planned to visit home regularly and join family conference calls to address her parents' needs. Katherine trusted that the other members of the family would help by becoming more involved in the care of her parents. It was up to them whether they wanted to keep the tradition of an annual family reunion alive; if so, they could take over the planning and execution of the event, and she'd be happy to attend. With a deep breath, she packed up her life and moved to England. She stopped worrying about whether her decision would make her un-popular with the family. Katherine's thoughts had been clouded by her desire to be needed and her out-of-balance sense of obligation to her relatives. Her self-talk focused on how others in the family might feel or think rather than on the responsibility she had to herself.

If you have assumed a similar role within your family, you might ask yourself questions like these:

- Why am I committed to taking better care of other people than of myself?

- To what degree is it healthy for both parties if I take care of another?

- Should I care for other people at the expense of my own self-care?

- Have I put on hold any aspects of my life that I no longer wish to defer?

Remember that being aware of your own needs and taking care of yourself is not selfish, nor does it indicate self-centeredness. It's loving.

CHILDLESS AND SUFFERING IN SILENCE

Michael and Janet

Michael and Janet grew up in a small factory town in Virginia. They attended the same schools and church, but it wasn't until high school that they became friends in the local 4-H club. During their childhood summers, they participated in local and regional county fairs, where Janet would sell canned goods and her own hand-knit baby blankets and sweaters. Michael would show his horses and give children pony rides.

Michael was one of six children raised on a ranch; the kids from youngest to oldest shared in the chores that kept the ranch running. Janet was the oldest child of four and watched over her younger siblings like a second mother. For her, having many children was just a matter of when. She and Michael shared a love of animals, country life, and homesteading, and grew to become the dearest of friends. Then one day Michael surprised and delighted Janet by asking her to their high school prom. Three years later, he proposed, and they were married before their twenty-second birthdays.

In their small town, just about everybody knows everybody else, and for Michael, Janet, and all their friends, marrying, buying a home with plenty of land, and having as many children as possible were extremely important goals. After ten years of marriage, Michael and Janet still hadn't conceived. At first they focused on the benefits of having plenty of time to enjoy life together, just the two of them. They worked hard, participated in community activities, and counted their blessings. But among their married friends—all now in their thirties—Michael and Janet were the only childless couple, although no one spoke openly of it. Nor did Janet and Michael speak of their fears and disappointment to each other. Neither of them wanted the other to feel blame or shame. Silently, their disappointment festered and the distance between them grew.

WHAT ARE THE SILENT AGREEMENTS?

Janet and Michael shared a very common silent agreement: **I won't talk about my disappointment if you don't talk about yours.** With every year that passed, they became more afraid that they might never have children together, and because each feared that the responsibility lay with himself or herself, they avoided bringing that truth to light. Ironically, their need to protect each other—thanks primarily to the guilt they felt for not being able to give the other something that mattered so deeply—led to a widening chasm between them. Michael began to feel like less of a man. He'd remain silent about this pain as he'd sit with his buddies at a tavern and listen to stories about their children. In their town, it was expected that a married man would eventually have children, and having a son was considered the greatest of blessings. Michael had a silent agreement with himself that **without a biological child, he wouldn't be fulfilled as a man.** Janet maintained a similar silent agreement with herself. As her insecurity grew, she began to feel that she was failing as a wife and as a woman. Her deepest fear was that Michael would eventually lose interest in her and leave. Their friends and relatives were participants in their silent agreements. By silently agreeing to **make life as bearable as possible for Michael and Janet by *not* raising the topic of having babies,** the people who loved them believed that they were being respectful and even merciful.

LIFTING THE SILENCE

Janet's sadness intensified, and she eventually stopped attending her knitting circles and family gatherings. Her friends and family watched her retreat and shared a variety of feelings ranging from concern to hurt. One Sunday during a church service, Janet was overcome with sadness, so she scheduled a meeting with her minister. They met the next day, and Janet began talking through a rush of tears. She told him about her withdrawal from friends, her frustration with her substantial weight gain, and most of all her fears about never being a mother or the kind of wife that Michael deserved. After calming down, she began to feel some relief, and her voice became clearer and stronger. Janet was finally able to say aloud that she wanted to be a parent, no matter what that meant. The minister suggested that she be honest with Michael about her feelings, and that after that conversation, the three of them should meet to discuss the options.

Janet realized that her disappointment, sense of failure, and fear of losing her marriage had sent her into depression. And she came to understand that her silence had contributed to her misery. "Why didn't I seek help earlier?" she wondered.

GOING FORWARD

Now that Michael and Janet were truly communicating, they were able to honestly talk about their options for the future. Janet's meeting with the minister had helped give her courage to talk about her feelings of shame, which opened the door for Michael to do the same. They soon met with their family doctor, who referred them to a fertility specialist, and when they discovered that in vitro fertilization was too expensive for them to contemplate, they began to discuss the possibility of adoption.

When friends or relatives have been suffering through silence, you may want to offer your support and help lift the silence that they are experiencing. Consider using some of these opening phrases:

- I'm always here for you if you need to talk.

- I will never discuss your private business with anyone without your permission.

- I think I've avoided talking about it because . . .

- Your happiness is really important to me. Whatever choice you make, I'm 100 percent behind you.

At the same time, if you are in a situation like Janet and Michael's, here are some questions that will help you navigate:

- Am I willing to find the compassion for myself right now during my time of greatest need?

- Am I committed to finding the courage I need to give up the silence that keeps me feeling lonely, miserable, and insecure?

- Am I willing to change my views about being an adoptive parent rather than a biological parent?

- Am I willing to let go of my need to be approved of by my family and community at the expense of my personal happiness?

- Which parts of my beliefs and customs should I keep? Which should I try to let go of?

A FEW TIPS

Family has an enormous range of definitions, and families are complex and full of unspoken opinions and hidden feelings. This very complexity lends itself to silent agreements, some lasting for generations. Keep in mind as you wend your way through this complicated landscape that sometimes you create silent agreements in the present and other times you step into agreements that have been growing for years. In any case, awareness is your best asset in your quest to lift the silence. Here are a few tips to help you do so:

- Try to talk about the issue sooner than later. To prepare for a potentially emotional and convoluted conversation, first write down your most important ideas and feelings. This helps you focus and gives you the comfort of knowing that you won't forget to address something that's important to you.

- Remind yourself that you're doing the right thing.

- Ask yourself: What's the worst thing that can happen by speaking truth? What is the best thing that can happen?

- If you find the idea of the first conversation particularly daunting, practice on someone you trust. It might sound like a silly exercise, but a practice run can give you confidence and clarity.

CHAPTER 7

SILENT AGREEMENTS IN
THE WORKPLACE

Every day in businesses all over the world, working professionals have thoughts like "Why aren't my people contributing more to the bottom line?" "Why does so much of the work fall on our team's shoulders?" "Why is my department expected to fix the company's problems when we didn't create them?" These internal conversations and the silent agreements that underlie them are ever present—while we're on phone calls, preparing documents, or attending meetings; even during our online communication. Within an office, workers relate to one another in a variety of ways. Supervisors try to motivate and inspire those working under them. Colleagues alternately support and undermine one another. Executives attempt to manage the bottom line while also dealing with a myriad of personality types. To varying degrees, members of the business, from clerk to CEO, are affected by these multifaceted interactions.

DIFFICULT PEOPLE IN THE OFFICE

We've all had the experience of working with someone whose behavior we find questionable, distasteful, or even intolerable. In such situations, we might complain or seek support from like-minded peers. We might address the situation with our superiors, have it out with the trouble-maker, or even begin to look for another job. But what if there's something else to consider? What if *you* are part of the problem?

The type of job you have dictates what kinds of equipment or supplies you're likely to take to work (a briefcase, a hard hat, a security badge, a laptop, your lunch), but no matter your profession, you always take your own personality. You also take your beliefs and expectations about the workplace as well as your personal idiosyncrasies. You might even tote your emotional and psychological difficulties. When you're dealing with a difficult person on the job, you're responding with your own silently held expectations about how this colleague is supposed to act, whether that colleague should keep his emotions under control (or acknowledge yours), and why you think your working environment should always be harmonious. Maybe you think that coworkers should always be polite and unemotional because that will allow for maximum productivity. But what if you have a coworker who expects to be free to blow off steam now and then with a loud, door-slamming exchange? These discrepancies in style can lead to conflict. But you need to accept that the conflict develops because of differing expectations from both of you.

When you encounter coworkers with difficult personalities, it's easy to blame problems on them, but it's more productive to identify and discuss the silent agreement that underlies the conflict between the two of you. Sometimes such conversations can be had after work or during your lunch hour, but timing is important. And a little preparation goes a long way. Consider these approaches:

1. Do your research. Talk to different people you trust to get different perspectives about your situation.
2. Think about how you'd like the situation to change, and determine which conversations you need to have to get there.
3. Understand that the person you're talking with may have just heard this for the first time. Nobody likes an ambush.
4. Be realistic. Rehearse the conversation before you talk to the person, and know that you may have to compromise.

THE PASSIVE-AGGRESSIVE COWORKER

Who, Me?

At a successful public relations firm, Danielle became very frustrated supervising Tara, an employee who had joined the firm nine months earlier. In many situations at work, Tara displays classically passive-aggressive behavior: She often remains silent after she's asked a question or given a direction, and when Danielle asks if Tara has heard her, Tara is likely to reply simply, "Yes, I did"—no elaboration, just the thud of a three-word answer. These interactions are frustrating for Danielle because she then has to ask again for a response, and the exchange feels like a ploy on Tara's part to shift control back to herself.

When Danielle needs to schedule a meeting with Tara, Tara usually finds all of Danielle's suggested meeting times inconvenient—another control move on Tara's part. If Danielle needs a report or document on her desk before the end of the day, Tara sends it just minutes before the close of business, after which time she'll dash out of the office, exhibiting a great show of anxiety. This prevents Danielle from being able to review Tara's work, ask questions about it, or have Tara correct it in time for a morning meeting the next day.

Danielle's efforts to discuss these issues with Tara are often fruitless. Tara has ready-made excuses for her behavior; she often defends herself by stating, "I always get my work done." She also says that she's intelligent enough to understand directions without needing a conversation about them and claims that her mad sprint at the end of the day is in line with her official quitting time, something she adheres to so she can pick up her child from the babysitter.

At the same time, Danielle has a habit of waiting until her frustration has hit a high point before confronting Tara with her concerns. Knowing that a blowup between two women in their mostly male work environment will not serve either of them, Danielle is careful to contain her growing frustration. As a result, she often walks away from these unsettled issues silently fuming. And sometimes she follows with some passive-aggressive behavior of her own, speaking curtly to Tara for days after these confrontations.

A passive-aggressive employee like Tara can be frustrating, not only because she behaves counterproductively but also because she doesn't take responsibility for her hostility. She might offer what she considers valid reasons for her behavior, but such justifications are rarely of help because they usually don't point to the core truth. Again, office relationships involve countless silent agreements, and when you're drawn into a conflict, one of the most proactive things you can do is consider whether you're part of one or more silent agreements underlying the problems.

WHAT ARE THE SILENT AGREEMENTS?

Danielle's and Tara's silent agreements are tainted by Tara's passive-aggressive nature and Danielle's tendency to fume rather than handle the situation like a confident supervisor with authority. Tara feels: **I have the right to autonomy, even in a workplace. Danielle is the boss, but she is not "above" me.** Danielle's silent agreement goes something like **I am a fair and reasonable supervisor, so when I ask an employee to do something, she needs to do it.**

Tara developed her passive-aggressiveness early in life as she tried not to disappear in the shadow of her cold, strict parents, who controlled her every decision—from what she could wear to what would be her college major. Tara resisted passive-aggressively by "accidentally" getting stains on her clothes, showing up to classes so late that she was locked out of the room, and hanging out with kids her parents disapproved of. As soon as she had enough money to move out, Tara left home.

Without realizing it, Danielle may have helped to trigger passive-aggressive responses from Tara by assuming that the hierarchy of the office was clear and non-negotiable, and would be adhered to. But Tara was more at ease with her previous boss's style: He would solicit Tara's opinions as they worked together on projects. This made it easier for her to accept direction without feeling that she was being controlled, as she had been so often while growing up.

Danielle played another part in this dynamic. When Tara would behave passive-aggressively, Danielle responded in a similar fashion. A look into Danielle's background helps explain some of this behavior. Danielle came from an organized household in which roles were clearly defined and carried out. Everyone knew their place, and the unspoken tenet was that this sense of order left no untidy details and nothing to discuss: "Just do your job." Danielle found comfort in this kind of order, so through school and into her professional life, she strove for clarity and efficiency. The problem was that her regimented supervisory style didn't work for Tara.

LIFTING THE SILENCE

These silent agreements need to be addressed and changed. Danielle as supervisor is in the best position to initiate a conversation that will clear the air and work toward a new understanding between the two women. Given the expectations that each woman brought to this work relationship, neither of them is likely to enjoy having this conversation. But as a supervisor, Danielle is responsible for making clear her expectations for her employees, and she has a responsibility to help her employees be effective and successful in the company.

Before having a conversation about their work relationship, both Danielle and Tara could first try to uncover the beliefs and expectations that they each bring to their work situation. Writing their observations is an effective exercise for this kind of discovery. Tara's description of how Danielle gives her direction might lead her to write something like this:

> When Danielle tells me to do something, she usually asks me over and over if I understand it, and then I end up annoyed and frustrated. **I expect** people to give me the room to do what I am asked because **I assume** that they can tell that I am intelligent enough to understand them the first time they ask. When a supervisor asks me a lot of questions about what I am doing, **I believe** it shows a lack of respect for my ability to figure things out on my own, something **I have hated** since growing up with my overbearing and controlling parents. **I believe** that a supervisee should not be treated like a child and that a supervisor does not have the right to hover over me.

When uncovering silent agreements in the workplace, it's helpful to note what you have observed and experienced that has made the conversation necessary, and it's also very effective if you also solicit the other person's point of view. So Danielle might say:

> It appears that we have different expectations about our working relationship. For instance, when it comes to scheduling our meetings, I usually offer you possible times to meet, and you usually respond by saying that none of them is convenient. On my end, I'm giving you times that I am **expecting** you to select from, but you end up offering different times for *me* to select from. I **assumed** you understood that I have the authority to set up meetings at times that I deem appropriate, not the other way around. I **have always believed** that when followed, business protocol like this scheduling method helps all of us to work more efficiently. I wonder how you view the situation and what your expectations have been about how the two of us should work together.

This conversation illustrates what Danielle has observed to be a point of conflict and reveals her own expectations, beliefs, and assumptions. Danielle indicates that she's aware of her own silent agreement as she mentions her belief about protocol—how it helps people to "work more efficiently."

Conversation starters you might use when having this kind of workplace conversation include:

1. I value . . .
2. I understand that we may see things differently . . .

3. I expected that you would (I would) . . .
4. I assumed that . . .
5. I believe that . . .
6. Does this make sense to you?
7. How do you see it?
8. I understand why you see it that way . . .
9. Going forward, I would expect . . .
10. Going forward, what would you expect?

GOING FORWARD

Tara's and Danielle's acknowledgment of their individual expectations can help them to come to an agreement that reflects both of their needs. Danielle can continue to establish protocol, but with elements that allow for Tara to work more independently. As the conversation progresses, Danielle might determine in which areas she expects Tara to function autonomously and in which scenarios she expects Tara to take more direction. If Tara knows that she'll be able to sometimes work independently, she may not be inclined to resist in her usual passive-aggressive way. By inquiring about and respecting the workplace needs of the people she supervises, Danielle will improve employee morale and performance. And she'll likely reduce her own frustration and passive-aggressive acting out. She can then be viewed as a fair and competent boss for whom others will *want* to work. Passive-aggressive behavior can be annoying and counterproductive, and the unclear nature of it can make getting to the heart of it difficult. One thing is clear: It needs to be met not with more passive-aggressiveness but with clear communication and action.

WHAT ABOUT YOU?

Can you try to identify which kinds of silent agreements may show up for you in the workplace? Some questions to ask yourself:

Are there any personality clashes between you and others at work?

Do you avoid dealing with those differences? How?

Is there anything about how you communicate or internalize your dissatisfaction with others that you want to change?

If so, are you willing to seek out new ideas, information, and resources to improve how you get along and communicate on the job?

Keep in mind that unrealistic assumptions and expectations abound in the workplace. And the truth is, you can work with someone for decades and never know much about them at all, certainly not what's important and how their silent agreements may form. If you keep this in mind and work on better communication, before and after silent agreements are formed, you may find that your workplace will become a more harmonious and productive place.

In Tara's case, others viewed her as difficult but competent, which blocked possible opportunities for promotion. She resented the promotions her coworkers were receiving and often failed to congratulate them. While Tara came across as a forceful personality, she was unsure about her ability to succeed. She had never received the support of her family, yet was the first in her family to graduate with an associate's degree from a community college.

Tara had always been more comfortable setting the bar far below what she was capable of achieving rather than disrupting how others in her close-knit family viewed her. Rather than challenging herself to exceed her goals, she stayed safely in her comfort zone. In so doing, she ensured that she would meet her goals but not fulfill her potential.

Tara began to recognize her silent agreement with herself when she attended a weekend workshop on career advancement. That weekend she realized that she had never allowed herself to explore her own dreams. Instead, she pretended to be satisfied with her job choice, but her resentment would often bleed through in her interactions with others.

After Tara joined a career support group that met weekly over the next few years, she began to flourish. She identified a new direction in her career that required a long-term commitment to return to college and realized that focusing on building her confidence and her relationships was key.

Here are some questions Tara might be asking herself now:

What additional support do I need to fulfill my dreams?

How do I stay authentic to myself during this change process?

What changes do I need to make every day to focus on my self-care and stay motivated?

How do I stay connected to my family without internalizing their low expectations?

How do I support the people I care about while protecting my dream?

THE NITPICKER

Nothing Is Ever Good Enough

Glen and Dave met through mutual friends, and when Glen established his new environmental sustainability firm, he knew that Dave would be a great addition to the team. The two men have been working together for two years, and while their entrepreneurial spirits are similar, the differences in their upbringings paved the way for the emergence of some silent agreements. Glen's hardworking but dysfunctional family had never expected him to amount to much, and they often told him so. They discouraged him from trying to go to college because "it's way over your head, it costs too much, and you'd be better off going straight to work like everyone else in the family." Dave, on the other hand, was raised by fast-thinking parents with boundless energy for adventure. His parents had no problem deciding to "go for it!" when they saw an opportunity. This attitude helped them to do extremely well in real estate. With such disparate childhoods, the two men invariably approached their business relationship differently.

Despite their firm's relaxed structure and the fact that Dave also invested money in the endeavor, Glen was the established senior partner. The new business was humming along, and they seemed poised for great success. But there was a problem: Glen had very specific ideas about how things should be done, and Dave wasn't meeting Glen's expectations. Because of Glen's need to control, Dave became more and more frustrated. He was growing weary of Glen's picky corrections of his emails and reports and even of Glen's critical commentary during meetings. Glen always critiqued with a smile, but Dave was often left feeling embarrassed and undermined. He didn't think that Glen's corrections made their business better, as they weren't about the quality of the work. Dave was now thinking about leaving the company.

WHAT ARE THE SILENT AGREEMENTS?

These men share a silent agreement but also have silent "addenda" that affect their work relationship. Their mutual silent agreement says, **We have a good opportunity to make something great of this company, and we're both going to do our best to make it happen.** This was a constructive agreement that served them well. But there were other agreements in play that led to problems. Dave's addendum: **I'm a competent, intelligent, and thoughtful partner, and I know what I'm doing. Glen needs to stay out of my way and let me do my job.** Glen's addendum: **My blood, sweat, and money are in this company, so Dave will understand my right to make sure that all operations, communications, and decisions meet my standards.**

It's easy to see why these agreements conflict. Having acknowledged only the part of their silent agreement that reflects their mutual desire to make the company a success, they both erroneously believed that they were in sync. Neither one agreed to the other's right to do it his way nor that the other's way might be superior to his own. If they don't communicate about their different beliefs in this regard, Glen might go on thinking that his approach is what's best for the company while Dave starts looking for a lawyer to help dissolve the partnership.

LIFTING THE SILENCE

How might these two colleagues approach the challenge of working together when one feels that his hovering perfectionism is warranted and the other feels that his competence is constantly being questioned? Their initial silent agreement is a healthy one; of course they both want to do their best to make the company a success. But by lifting the silence, they'll be in a position to revise the agreement to include some specifics. They have to uncover their beliefs and expectations about what represents "good" and "good enough" work, and they need to explore at what point picky perfectionism results in diminishing returns. Because they are partners and equals, it's appropriate for either one of these men to initiate the conversation. As always, the most effective conversation will involve each genuinely listening to the other. And as always, such conversations will be greatly helped by the use of phrases like:

1. I value . . .
2. To me, this partnership means . . .
3. I expected . . .

4. I've avoided talking about this because . . .
5. Going forward, I want . . .
6. I can understand why you see it that way.
7. I hear you, but I see it differently.
8. Is this clear to you?
9. What is your perspective on it?
10. Where do we go from here?

WHAT ABOUT YOU?

For many of us, work is about a whole lot more than making money. Take a few minutes to think about what your job or career means to you. Consider your work-related beliefs, values, and ways of relating to others to identify whether you have more attention to pay in this area.

You might ask yourself these questions about your relationship dynamics in the workplace:

How do I receive and respond to feedback about my work performance?

If I could change anything about how I perform in the workplace, what would it be?

How do my early family dynamics shape how I conduct myself in work relationships?

How do my attitudes about competition affect the way I see my coworkers?

How do I deal with conflict at work?

Do I judge others as winners or losers? If so, how does that affect how I treat my coworkers as well as my clients?

Remember that you represent a significant part of every relationship that you're in, so if there's a problem, you're part of that, too.

As we know, the emotional intelligence required to shore up our relationships with our business partners is quite similar to that necessary in our relationships with our life partners. Glen and Dave had conflicting scripts for success. Unfortunately, they were more focused on the other's faults than on the benefits that each brought to the business.

BUSINESS MEETS PLEASURE
Romance and Sex in the Workplace

Oh, boy. When sex and romance enter the workplace, the opportunity for complications is unlimited. Often such relationships involve expectations, hopes, and fears that are common in relationships outside the professional realm, but a work setting can add the elements of secrecy and risk. And such liaisons often breed gossip, silent agreements, and conflicts. When silent agreements about how these relationships are supposed to operate don't match, the resulting behaviors don't align either, so problems are bound to emerge.

If you venture into work/romance territory, you likely

have a silent agreement not only with your romantic interest but also one with yourself. You might be telling yourself things like "My new lover and I are discreet enough that people won't know what we're up to"; "Neither of us will say a word to other colleagues, so we'll be safe from office gossip"; "This relationship is so exciting that it's worth the risks." These kinds of silent agreements allow you to enter risky relationships and claim little or no responsibility when they're exposed. And office romances are quite often exposed.

Jana and Carlos were colleagues who were attracted to each other the moment they met. They flirted in the elevator, in the kitchen, and in hallways. Jana knew that a romantic entanglement at work would be tricky, but soon it was clear that the two of them were not going to hold back much longer. During the office Christmas party, the mistletoe gave them an easy excuse for their first kiss. Then they disappeared into the kitchen to refill the cookie tray and *wham!* Their hands were all over each other.

They worked in different departments, she in operations and he in sales, and they teased each other throughout the day with steamy texts and sexy phone calls. For months, they had a thrilling affair, meeting after work and sharing weekends filled with laughter and sexy role play. He was divorced. She was "semi-engaged" to a man who lived across the country. Without seeming to notice, they created a silent agreement about the rules for their relationship.

Six months passed, and it was clear to both of them that while they enjoyed their trysts, they weren't in it for the long term. Jana was only twenty-four and in a year or two intended to relocate to California. As a recently divorced father of a young daughter, Carlos wasn't ready for a serious relationship. Both of them expected that their office romance would fade naturally, and when it did, they went back to being just colleagues but ones with luscious memories.

Then one day Jana overheard two coworkers gossiping about her relationship with Carlos. "Carlos hates drama and didn't want to deal with his ex-wife's jealousy," one of them whispered to the other. "She uses the daughter as a weapon, so he decided it was easier to just cut it off with Jana." Jana was furious that Carlos had revealed their secret, so she confronted him. "You've got to be kidding me! Really? Bragging?? Are you in high school?" Then Carlos reacted with anger of his own. "Do you think that people didn't know we were together and that it wasn't obvious when we stopped? Anyway, I'm free to talk about my personal life with my friends."

WHAT ARE THE SILENT AGREEMENTS?

This is a clear case of mismatched silent agreements about an in-office romance. They had each "agreed" to their own version of **Because we work together, we'll be discreet about this relationship**. But they hadn't agreed about what that discretion included and excluded. To Jana, the agreement meant that they wouldn't discuss their relationship with *anyone* in the company. But Carlos trusted his friends with his secrets, even if those friends were also his colleagues. Because neither knew of the other's expectations, they each believed that they shared a definition of what discretion involved. For Jana, Carlos's sharing with his friends was a breach of the agreement. For Carlos, Jana's response was naive. As is always the case with silent agreements, each person brought expectations and beliefs from their pasts into the present.

Carlos grew up in a loud, gregarious household where secrets were quickly uncovered—usually followed by a lot of teasing and laughter. Thus, as a child Carlos learned that most "secrets" were to be shared. He thought that as long as he and Jana didn't make a show of their relationship, he was being subtle enough, and he believed in sharing his personal life with his friends.

Jana grew up in a family in which she learned to keep her feelings to herself. Her family members were constantly in one another's business, and she hated it. After her father cheated on her mother, the sad and sordid story seemed to frame every accusation and pitying glance from aunts to godmothers. She promised herself that her private business would remain private, and it did—at least until Carlos came along. What she considered exposure left her feeling more shame and guilt than she expected.

LIFTING THE SILENCE

Although they had already ended the romantic relationship, Carlos and Jana would still be well served by a conversation that could help preserve their work relationship. Jana could make clear that given her graduate school aspirations, she's depending on a positive recommendation. "Not afraid of an office romance" isn't the kind of commentary she wants following her to the next step on her career path. Carlos could agree not to discuss the relationship further with his office friends. And Carlos and Jana might agree that should anyone at work ask about their relationship, they'll answer with a simple "We're just friends." The experience may have taught them both a valuable lesson: Next time, establish the ground rules early and out loud.

ALL IS FAIR IN LOVE AND WORK

Nyla and Blair

Nyla and Blair have been working for the same company for five years. They have each moved through different departments as they gradually worked their way up the corporate ladder. One day the managers of each of their departments announced an initiative that would require Nyla's and Blair's departments to work together over the next eighteen months. It was an exciting opportunity for both of them to demonstrate their skills and competencies, and the possibility of heading a newly formed department when the initiative was completed ignited their interest. The two worked together during many meetings and through several late nights. Sometimes they shared a company cab home or went out together for a late-night drink.

On one of those nights, Nyla confessed that she was attracted to Blair, and to her surprise, Blair admitted to having similar feelings. These two savvy women knew better than to try to have a workplace romance without spelling out their expectations clearly and directly, and after several conversations doing just that, they decided to pursue their interest in each other, with strict guidelines about leaving their personal relationship outside of work. They understood that the company looked down on workplace romance, and they were also aware of the possible bias against same-sex relationships at their conservative workplace.

This worked well, and they continued to interact at work while maintaining a loving and passionate relationship outside the office. Both were very discreet and fully aware of the consequences if their relationship were to be discovered. Eventually Nyla moved in with Blair, although she kept her own apartment for appearances.

The project went well. Finally, when the initiative had been completed, Blair's manager called her into a meeting. She congratulated Blair on her contribution to the project and told her how impressed she was with her work. Her manager then offered Blair the position as head of the new department. She noted that Blair would preside over a group of her coworkers who would be culled from the two departments involved with the project. Among those would be her girlfriend, Nyla.

Blair could hardly contain her excitement that evening when she invited Nyla to join her at their favorite restaurant and told her of her new position that was to be announced later that week. Nyla was happy for Blair and let her know with enthusiasm, ordering champagne and telling her how much she deserved it. Blair thanked her but wondered aloud if Nyla felt at all uncomfortable with Blair's being her new boss. Nyla replied emphatically, "Absolutely not. You worked hard, and I think they made a great choice. I plan to support you in your new role." Then

Nyla asked Blair, "What about you? Will you be able to assess my work objectively? And how will you feel when I ace the hell out of *my* new role and get promoted to the next best thing at the company?" They both got a good laugh out of this, and each knew that while Nyla was joking, she was serious about doing her best and climbing the ranks. For both of them, it was all just fine.

WHAT IS THE SILENT AGREEMENT?

Even in this example of harmony in the midst of a situation that could be rife with emotional complications, a silent agreement was at play. How was it possible that Blair and Nyla were able to avoid the potential damage to their personal and professional relationship? Their silent agreement was perfectly aligned with their beliefs and expectations. It said, **We will embark on this relationship and keep our professional and personal lives separate. Our personal relationship is a priority, but it cannot be allowed to interfere with our individual efforts at work.**

Both women entered the relationship with a foundation of communication, and many of their relationship rules were clearly stated, including the tenet that they would continue to communicate often and directly about how they were doing. Most important, they silently agreed that their relationship was a priority but that it had nothing to do with their individual workplace ambitions or efforts. Each understood the other's ambitions and had no expectation that having an "office relationship" would mean limiting themselves professionally.

Both of these women were strong and confident and

enjoyed these qualities in each other. Neither was threatened by the other's goals, and both could be loving and supportive of the other's success. Rather than view themselves as competitors, they believed that they were a team of smart, successful women who had a long life of accomplishments and love to look forward to.

MORE THAN A MENTOR
Charisse and Daxon

Charisse was a new associate in her law firm and was fiercely independent. Her superiors noticed immediately that she was smart and diligent, an exceptional worker. Daxon, one of the partners, took a particular liking to her. On one occasion, he invited her to his office to review her progress and talk about the path to becoming a partner in the firm. He said that he'd like to mentor her and would meet with her on a regular basis to offer advice and support as she moved up the ladder.

Charisse was ambitious, so this was very good news. She'd heard rumors about Daxon being a bit of a ladies' man, so she wondered if he was going to come on to her. She decided that if he did, she'd go for it. He was single and attractive, and she was eager to get on the fast track to her goals. Anyway, she didn't have time to look for a boyfriend, so if things moved that way it might be nice to have the companionship and a no-strings-attached sex partner who might spoil her.

Along with the mentoring, they enjoyed an entire year

of secret rendezvous and lavish weekends. Still, Charisse was shocked when "Dax" told her that he was in love with her and wanted them to become an exclusive couple. She couldn't believe that this highly accomplished middle-aged man actually believed that she wanted a long-term relationship with him. He was a colleague, he was fourteen years her senior, and the real love in her life at this point was her career. The word around the office was that he'd had this kind of fling before—didn't he understand how these things worked?

Dax was surprised by Charisse's refusal because he wasn't used to being turned down, not in any aspect of his life. And he had worked carefully to make sure that she would be considered for the promotion that she very much wanted. But he was also terribly disappointed. How could she not share his feelings? Didn't she understand that their becoming a real couple would work to her advantage, given that Dax was a senior partner in the firm and knew its landscape better than anyone else?

WHAT ARE THE SILENT AGREEMENTS?

Both Charisse and Dax believed that they were having a mature adult relationship without compromising themselves or each other. But their unspoken agreement didn't match the beliefs and expectations that underscored the agreement. Dax was thinking, **As I mentor Charisse, I'll also get to know her romantically, and if it becomes something serious, that will be a good thing that we can both commit to.** Charisse was thinking, **Dax will mentor me,**

and in the process we'll have a fling that involves each of us getting what we need from the arrangement with no strings attached.

People who engage in these types of relationships often forget that while it's a "work romance," the relationship is still with a whole person, one who may have hopes for a relationship that extends well beyond either of their careers with the company. When issues like insecurity, possessiveness, jealousy, and most of all, mismatched expectations are part of a romantic relationship that overlaps a professional one, things can get very complicated. Given that careers are often at stake, silent agreements embedded in workplace romances are best made explicit as soon as possible.

LIFTING THE SILENCE

When Dax finally faced the fact that Charisse would never jump back into his arms, he knew something had to change. He realized that Charisse was not the only one who was married to work. He discovered another silent agreement with himself, which was the belief that success would make everything else better. There was nothing more important to him than achieving success at his Fortune 500 company.

After the breakup, Dax spent months trying to avoid his feelings by escaping into fifteen-hour workdays; all that mattered was the company. Exhausted and unable to concentrate or rest, he realized that work had taken over his life. That's when he knew he *had* to change. So, recognizing that the damage had been done, he picked himself up, licked his wounds, and wondered who his best self was if he wasn't working. In desperation, he opened up to one of his few close work associates, who suggested Dax take a few days off and go to a health retreat that had helped him through a prior rough patch.

Dax went on the retreat and experienced a break-through. He realized that throughout his life, work had meant everything to him. Now, instead of being in control and dominating his competitors, he knew his dependency on work had the power to destroy him. He could also see that "falling in love" with Charisse, no matter how pain-ful, was a sign to change and create a more balanced life. As difficult as it was, he accepted the help he needed to retool and begin to incorporate daily physical and mental exercises to help him relax, regain his confidence, develop new interests, and modify his work schedule so that he could make time for self-exploration.

It can be a huge problem when one partner is in love and the other isn't and doesn't want to be. When such an imbalance in love also involves work, the situation can threaten professional reputations and livelihoods. It's obvi-ous that the imbalance in Dax and Charisse's silent agree-ments isn't going to allow for long-term harmony for this couple. Charisse's desire for no strings cannot be aligned with Dax's expectations for a more serious commitment. And their disparate positions—in the firm, where *he* has the power and she doesn't; and in love, where *she* has the power and he doesn't—will make their differing goals and desires even more challenging. If these two can un-cover and communicate their very different expectations, perhaps they can find a happy middle ground where they can continue to work together despite ending the romantic part of their relationship. Charisse shouldn't be surprised if this doesn't happen; even successful middle-aged men can suffer from broken hearts.

Clearly, Dax and Charisse need to have a courageous conversation. Because this is both a personal and a workplace conversation, their discussion must address both elements. They might begin the conversation by saying, "I value our relationship and the bond we've developed, but I think we view the nature of it differently. I may not have been very clear about my expectations for us. Let's talk and try to understand where each of us is coming from." With this opening, the notion of differences is acknowledged right away, as is the goal of the conversation—understanding each other. In their conversation, they can use language that clarifies their assumptions and expectations and that also invites the other party to do the same:

1. Does this make sense to you now?
2. Does this come as a surprise?
3. What were your expectations?
4. I understand why you see it that way.
5. How do you see us going forward with these differences?

GOING FORWARD

This conversation isn't likely to be a comfortable one, but if Dax and Charisse are honest about how they feel about the relationship and each other, they'll develop an understanding of each other. In couples with mismatched silent agreements about the basic definition of the relationship, the more invested party often ends up feeling misled or betrayed, but if they can discuss the beliefs and expectations that led to the misalignment, there's a chance that both parties can walk away feeling understood. If that happens, there's a greater chance of an amicable relationship going forward. While Dax's and Charisse's wishes might not be in alignment in the romance department, the self-awareness and clarity they can gain from an open discussion about the challenges and risks of workplace romance can be invaluable now and in the future.

WHAT ABOUT YOU?

To help make sure that your professional life and personal life balance in a healthy way, consider these questions:

Do I believe that my work life is more important than my personal life? How much do they overlap?

Am I spending enough time with friends and family? When was the last time I reached out to those I care about?

Do I find myself waking up in the middle of the night trying to solve job-related problems and then have a hard time falling back to sleep?

Do I expect that work success will bring me happiness? Am I pursuing happiness outside of work?

Have I neglected important aspects of a balanced life, such as exercise, downtime, hobbies, and getaways, in the interest of being more professionally productive?

Has work become the only source of personal relationships? Where else can I make them?

What changes do I need to make to have more balance in my everyday work life?

How do I define success? What am I willing to do to achieve it?

How does the income I earn warrant the time I spend working and any sacrifices my job might call for?

There are countless scenarios that lead to silent agreements in the workplace. Some have been addressed in this chapter, while others involve hiring and firing, work reviews, nepotism, substance abuse, confidentiality—the list is as long as a corporate roster. Work relationships can be very significant because they're tied to important elements of our lives—income, ambition, and creative and intellectual growth. As with our personal and sexual relationships, work relationships are affected by our personal histories, values, and expectations. We bring a whole range of factors into the office that will become part of our professional associations and that will lead to silent agreements.

A word about ethnic, cultural, gender, and generational differences is warranted here. All of these areas can be rife with silent agreements simply because they can so powerfully influence a person's upbringing and worldview, as well as their assumptions and expectations of others. Thus, in a diverse workplace there is a high potential for a wide variety of mismatched silent agreements. In many respects these areas and the silent agreements that often come into play deserve a book of their own to do justice to their importance. For now, it can't be emphasized enough that a workplace that doesn't recognize the silent agreement conflicts that can brew—for example, between a millennial new hire and a middle-aged manager, a transgender worker and her straight, conservative office mate, an African American sales director and her Middle Eastern male assistant—is a workplace headed for trouble. A concerted effort to identify and communicate about the silent agreements that may surround these differences will go a long way to boosting morale and maintaining a healthy and productive work environment. The approaches we have outlined can help.

At the same time, when you encounter difficult personalities at work, or if you're involved in a workplace romance that's becoming complicated, it's helpful to remind yourself that silent agreements can be present even though your initial reaction might be to blame the problems on the other person. While many of us generally have difficulty communicating about awkward situations, this aversion can be much more intense in the workplace. But the story remains the same: If you can acknowledge the desires, the beliefs, and even the baggage you're bringing to the table, that awareness will put you in a good position to begin to address your part in your professional silent agreements.

CHAPTER 8

SILENT AGREEMENTS ABOUT HEALTH

Many health-related silent agreements reflect the belief that if we don't talk about it, we won't have to admit our fear that there's a lot about our health that we are either unable or unwilling to control. In this chapter, we address the pitfalls of being silent about our own health and about the health practices of others. We sometimes tell people we're fine when we know we're far from it. Rather than admit that we've begun couples therapy, we might tell our friends that on Tuesdays we're "taking an art class." Sometimes we simply become fatigued by the truth and choose to tell a different health story, as does Janice, a single mother with a sick child. She can't afford to skip another day of work but has no one to watch her asthmatic seven-year-old son. She'll tell her boss, "I can't come in today because I'm having another migraine." There are times when we think it's just too difficult or expensive to follow a doctor's advice, so we silently agree to manage the health situation ourselves and hope for the best, even when our instincts nag that we're putting ourselves in jeopardy. Have you ever rescheduled a physical exam for a seemingly frivolous reason? Have you ever opted to forgo a recommended medication because you hoped you would get better without it? Or ignored a symptom because you just didn't want to know?

There are also the health-related silent agreements that remain silent because we just don't want to stir up conflict or cause anyone to feel uncomfortable about the choices they've made. We don't speak up about our friend's smoking habit. We make no mention of the fact that our favorite cousin—with a family history of heart disease—has gained fifty pounds in the past two years. We tell ourselves that these people are adults, they make their own choices, and we have no business telling another adult what to do.

Sometimes a silent agreement develops gradually and along the way creates so many potential landmines that we find ourselves tiptoeing through our lives to avoid them. And silent agreements are often found in unexpected places. For the Johnson family, they were located in the kitchen.

FOOD, FAMILY, AND FICTION

The Johnson Family

Paula was a parent committed to the health of her family, a family that included a teenage daughter who spent a lot of her free time in the kitchen. Paula grew up in poverty, and even though her family had little to no money, her mother would use extra change to buy flour, sugar, and eggs and would try to bake away the family's woes. Giving away delicious homemade treats filled her mother with pride and made her feel generous despite her poverty. For her skill at baking, she became the envy of the community, thanks primarily to her homemade pocketbook rolls that seemed to melt on the tongue.

Now the family's culinary tradition had been passed on to Paula's daughter, Nia. Over the years, Nia became a proficient baker who proudly shared her creations, and this ability earned her the appreciation and admiration of countless friends and relatives. It also led her to be forty-five pounds overweight at the age of sixteen. Unlike other teenagers who dashed after school to clubs and team practices, Nia rushed home to the kitchen, where her grandmother taught her baking techniques and family secrets. Every Sunday, Nana would say, "I have your apron in here. Let's get the rolls into the oven."

Nia wasn't obsessed with clothes shopping or the latest dance craze, as were so many of her peers. Baking was her pastime, her passion, and her escape. One day during a routine physical exam, a doctor told Nia and Paula that Nia was medically obese and had type 1 diabetes. Nia sat on the exam table and cried softly. Paula assured her daughter they would come up with an exercise routine and would manage her medicine and diet together. But Paula refused to discuss the obvious connection between her daughter's weight gain and her habit of baking foods loaded with fat and sugar. Although Paula recognized that diabetes is a serious disease, she thought baking was an important hobby for Nia and felt most connected to Nia in the kitchen. Most of all, she didn't want to discourage her daughter's passion. She often reminded her daughter that she was a beautiful young woman, but secretly she hoped that Nia would want to lose weight on her own. The family kept silent for weeks following the doctor's visit, and no one pushed for more exercise. As Nia's weight continued to increase, her immediate family retreated more and more into their own silent denial of their involvement in the development of a very dangerous problem.

WHAT ARE THE SILENT AGREEMENTS?

This family's silent agreement is generations old. For centuries, baking has been an admirable way to exhibit talent and skills and to create something delicious for everyone to share. The fact that Nia was following a family tradition delighted them all, despite the fact that it had become detrimental to her health. The family's silent agreement was that **even though it jeopardized her well-being, Nia's baking should continue because it had been great for her self-esteem and continued a family tradition.** The agreement rested on the belief that baking is a great bonding mechanism and the rationalization that the Johnson women had always been "big-boned." Nia had a silent agreement that **as long as she kept the Johnson cooking tradition alive, she'd be loved and valued by her family members.** No matter how much teasing she put up with in school, her family was proud of her, so she also silently agreed **to do her best to ignore the taunts from the girls at school who mocked her weight.**

All the family members were trying to protect Nia, and they told themselves that her obesity wasn't really a disease. They loved that the latest generation of the family was upholding the tradition of the importance of food in the household, and anyway, none of the elders knew how to help someone with eating or weight issues. They were all complicit—parents, grandparents, and extended family. No one felt comfortable intervening. Certainly not Nana, who treasured the time she and her granddaughter spent together in the kitchen. But the adults in the family could see that there was a problem, and the time to hide behind tradition was over.

LIFTING THE SILENCE

The road to recovery for Nia began with her parents acknowledging their complicity in creating the problem. This required some courageous conversations, starting with the parents, then expanding to include grandparents, Nia herself, and potentially anyone that might be considered to be part of Nia's inner circle, such as her best friends. These people constitute her *circle of influence*. It's often a revelation to people that their own values have an influence on the well-being of others, but it is so. We project these values through our behaviors, and often the projected ideals and beliefs make others feel, react, and behave in certain ways that aren't necessarily in their best interests. After all, in many ways these ideals may come from our unspoken needs that we somehow end up forcing on others.

So how does a family like the Johnsons rescue itself from its predicament? One way is to start using

I-statements when family members talk about Nia's health. An effective way to structure this kind of sharing is to use some form of "and this is how it makes me feel" within each statement. Some examples:

As a mother, Paula needs to explain how Nia's health is affecting her by telling the family what she experienced in relation to food as she grew up. "I grew up without enough food to eat, and I'm coming to understand that this created a fear of not having enough. The fear drives me to make sure there's always enough food for everyone at all times. I believe that my fear of living in poverty has caused a blindness to the impact of Nia's constant cooking and baking. This makes me feel like a culprit in my daughter's health issues." Go, Mama! Any time we look within to uncover our old beliefs and expectations, we clear the way to truly see where our responsibility lies when it comes to keeping secrets.

Mack, the father: "I wanted to believe that cooking was making my baby happy and that's what mattered most. I didn't want to deal with Nia's increasing weight. Now I feel that I kind of buried my head in the sand." How often do we cover our eyes to avoid the bright glare of truth? Probably more than we're willing to admit, and maybe even more than we know. Mack's statement reveals his desire to protect and provide for his family. He says exactly what he felt and explains what he did and why. That's very productive communication when trying to uncover silent agreements.

Nia: "Sometimes I think I should be hanging out with other girls, not cooking all the time. It feels awful to be obese and to know that I have diabetes. Part of me wants to hide from the uncool facts of my life by staying where I know I'm a success, in the kitchen. This makes me want to cook even more. But I also like being the one who keeps up a great family tradition. I really don't want to quit it. I know I need to turn this around, but I'm not sure how to do it, and I need my family's help." A teenager who can articulate this perspective is expressing very mature thoughts about her responsibility in the development of her problem and her need for help in solving it. Given that hers isn't a problem that's simple or quickly solved, Nia will need to summon the discipline to change her habits one day at a time. That takes courage and real, lasting help.

Nana: "I just want to spend time with my granddaughter teaching her the way to cook the old recipes. I don't think she should be punished for liking to eat, and I don't want to lose this shared experience that means so much to both of us. I'm not sure what to do about it." Nana didn't appear to grasp the enormity of the problem. If Nana doesn't help Nia to cook less and bake less (or at least with less fat and sugar), Nia probably won't be able to follow through and improve her health. Nana is more than

Nia's grandmother, she's Nia's closest friend, and significant change can be very difficult if our best friend, spouse, or other close loved ones don't think the change is necessary. Realizing that she doesn't have the answers, Nana looks to others in the family to help her understand what needs to happen to help give their beloved Nia the healthiest possible future. Those of us who want to help and aren't sure what to do can tear a page out of Nana's playbook.

GOING FORWARD

If you had been a member of the Johnson family, what would you have done? You might have begun by finding a way to understand your role in the dynamic of your family and by thinking about healthier ways to express your family's traditions. The Johnson family chose to channel their energy in a new direction. They began to make memories by spending time together doing activities focused on fun, play, and sports, not on food and cooking, particularly baking. Because cooking had become the central bonding activity, they realized they needed to replace it with a healthy one.

Together they agreed to learn more about nutrition and planned family meetings to divide the responsibilities of cooking and baking between all the members of the family. Mack committed to making shopping lists and doing the family grocery shopping. Nana said she would work on menus with Nia and run them by Paula. Paula committed to cooking on the weekends and on two of five weeknights. Dividing these responsibilities allowed each of them to actively take steps to change the role of food in their family's life as well as their relationship to it. Paula shopped for healthy cookbooks and joined Nia in looking for recipes for baked goods that called for healthier, less fattening ingredients. Nia began to enjoy experimenting, trying to create healthy treats that came as close as possible to the flavors and consistencies of the fattier versions. With a two-pronged approach—education and new kinds of cooking—the original silent agreement became an explicit open and engaged agreement that the entire family participated in. The new agreement is **to share the responsibility as a family for incorporating healthy food, cooking, and baking into their lives and to augment their food-based traditions with new traditions that fulfill the need for family bonding.** This freed Nia from carrying the Johnson food tradition on her own and made more space for her to have some teenage fun.

As you read through the Johnsons' story, you may be thinking about similar food-linked silent agreements in your family. To help you figure out the role they're playing in your life and health, consider these kinds of questions to lift the silence:

- What is the health history of your family relative to food? Who knows it and who doesn't?

- What was your childhood experience with food? How has that flowed into your adulthood?

- Is your family silent about eating and weight issues? If so, why?

- Have diabetes or other diet-related diseases affected the quality of life for any members of your family?

- What beliefs, assumptions, and expectations are reflected in your family's traditions about food? Are any of these present in your own approach to food?

- Which family members, including you, are most likely to hold on to family food traditions? Who is more likely to let them go? Why?

- What family stories or traditional activities can elders share to cultivate family time that centers on relationships rather than on food?

- Would you be willing to speak up and ask for help if any members of your family seemed to be eating themselves to death or, conversely, deliberately starving themselves?

If you do your best to answer these questions thoughtfully, you'll be on the road to uncovering the silent agreements about food and health that you have internalized and continue to manifest. And if you're able to discuss these kinds of questions with members of your family, you'll be opening a very important door to understanding how their silent agreements about food can limit their ability to live their healthiest lives.

DOUBLE TROUBLE
Heart Disease and a Broken Heart

In her early childhood, Mary was told that she had a heart murmur, but some years later a heart specialist diagnosed an enlarged heart. Then, as she was learning to accept her physical predicament, she experienced a trauma of unthinkable proportions: She walked into the family's kitchen and found her alcoholic father dead on the floor. She was only six when it happened, so her recounting of the story is spotty, but she begins by describing her terror as she heard her mother scream. She ran in the direction of the awful sounds and found her father facedown near the refrigerator. She remembers her mother's tortured attempts to communicate—with tears streaming down her cheeks, she could emit only voiceless cries. Mary felt a wrenching pain in her chest and remained motionless for what felt like hours.

Unfortunately, it wasn't until Mary's adult years that she sought professional help to deal with the emotional scars caused by her childhood trauma. After her father's death, she became the "quiet child" in the family, while her older sister and brother remain engaged "at an appropriate level," as her aunts would explain. Mary was treated delicately, as if she couldn't bear the weight of life's difficulties. When her mother's sisters would speak about Mary's father, she would often hear, "Please keep your voice down. We don't want to upset Mary."

Mary developed anxiety and depression during her college years. There were times she felt so isolated and shut down that she spent entire days without leaving her room. At one point her roommates became alarmed and notified the health center. Finally she had to take a semester off. She managed to earn a degree, but after graduation, Mary wasn't prepared to face the daily struggles stemming from her trauma. After many years of suffering from anxiety, depression, and small and large fears, Mary told herself, "I'm depressed from the trauma and will bear the burden for the rest of my life." Mary assumed that feeling low was simply to be part of her life, now and forever. To that end, she went on to share the story of her "double heartbreak" with every man she dated, hoping that he had a big enough heart to stay with her, and believing that nobody would.

WHAT IS THE SILENT AGREEMENT?

The first part of Mary's silent agreement was: **When I reveal my trauma and depression, people will pity me and will see me only as my illness.** The second part of her silent agreement was that **she believed she had to live with great and consistent emotional pain, and that this was going to be the whole of her life.** Mary's wounds continued to be an emotional trigger; her heart disease and the tragic way her father died caused her shame and pain every day. Not even medication helped. She feared that depression was the cloud that would hang over her forever, and that possibility brought with it more vulnerability and the risks of crushing disappointment. She was also acutely conscious of her family's fatigue from watching her roller-coaster life, her hopes rising when new therapeutic solutions were proposed, followed by disappointment and more depression.

She suspected they'd be happier if she accepted a life of quiet resignation.

LIFTING THE SILENCE AND GOING FORWARD

Mary desperately needed a route out of her hopelessness, and toward that end, her family could offer no answers. But almost as powerful as being able to change a situation is the ability to change your perception of the situation. Working with a good therapist could help her to make such a shift, so she could begin to view herself as a person with a life much greater than her symptoms.

As is true of any of us facing complex health challenges, Mary had a lot to consider. She realized that her constant preoccupation with what she perceived as her deficits did not help her mental health. She needed to reassess who she wants to be; it was time to become the boss of her situation rather than being ruled by anxiety and depression. In addition to continuing therapy, she could benefit from countless helpful resources while incorporating positive practices into her life—acupuncture, yoga, prayer, meditation, and nutrition modification.

If you have a silent agreement anything like Mary's, consider asking yourself some of these questions:

1. What am I doing to make people view me as a victim of my health challenges?
2. What steps can I take to stop viewing myself as a victim?
3. How can I see myself as being healthy and whole enough to have a happy life?

4. How can I learn that I'm entitled to a life not defined by my health burdens?

5. What is it going to take for me to live a life focused on wellness?

The challenge we all face is figuring out what is at the root of our painful lives. Mary knows. And while that doesn't stop the cycle of moods or shift the course of her cardiovascular disease, it starts to open her agreement with herself ever so slightly. We all need to allow the awareness of our health challenges to sink in. Maybe if we shift our focus to some celebration of our whole self, we can reject the sad, hopeless fear of being sick and notice that maintaining the silent agreement may no longer be needed or helpful.

CAREGIVER, HUSBAND, DIRECTOR, AND HEALTH RISK

Joe Martin Lewis

Entering middle age can be daunting even for the most organized and optimistic person, but if you're positioned squarely in the so-called sandwich generation, you may be raising children while also caring for an elderly parent. That's where middle-aged Joe Martin Lewis, vice president of a successful public relations firm, found himself. And every day the pressure was increasing.

Joe had been doing a good job of balancing the demands of being a good parent, husband, and company man, and he also paid close attention to his own health.

He had always felt responsible for those around him, and his expectations of himself were high. Then his mother was diagnosed with ulcers, glaucoma, and Alzheimer's disease, and true to form, Joe jumped in to take care of her as well. The pace of his life became exhausting, and on many days, he was left feeling devastated and untethered. For many years, Joe had been able to rely on his father to care for his mother. Now his father had to deal with his own declining health, which left the responsibility to Joe. He began to have difficulty sleeping, eating, and concentrating. In the office he used to be able to focus completely on a project, but then the calls from his father began coming in two and three times a day: "Your mother's memory is getting worse." Joe decided that the best way to manage his parents' declining health was to move his parents in with his immediate family, so he did. With this change in his household configuration, he often had to stay up late finishing projects.

As his caregiver responsibilities expanded, Joe's wife and kids began to feel that there was a distance growing between him and them. His wife said that his personality was changing, that he seemed distracted and short-tempered. Joe began to develop stomach problems so intense that pills to combat acid reflux became part of his regular diet. Then came the headaches. And then back pain, which at times was excruciating.

WHAT ARE THE SILENT AGREEMENTS?

Joe's silent agreement with himself was: **In order to be a truly good husband, father, and son, I have to take care of**

everyone important in my life while putting myself last. The Joe Way is to say yes first and then figure out how to manage what he just committed to. He would tell himself that his life isn't his own "for now" but will be again once everyone else is settled and secure. Meanwhile, his wife's silent agreement was: **If I keep my eye on Joe and assure myself that he's okay, I won't have to worry whether he's in over his head.** But she did begin to worry. And for some time they just didn't talk about it. They discussed the details of their lives and simply breezed past the impact his overload was having on their marriage, their children, and most of all, his health.

LIFTING THE SILENCE AND GOING FORWARD

Joe was good at juggling a lot of responsibilities. He liked knowing what the next task was, but he wasn't so good at talking about being overburdened, even to the degree that his obligations negatively affected his health. For Joe, it was easier just to move on to the next task. But then it became time for some important conversations. There are many questions relative to work-life balance, caregiving, and everyone's health that could help Joe and his wife sort through what was happening. For example:

- Is there a way to share some of the caregiving so that Joe isn't the only one carrying the load?

- How might Joe restructure his work so that he will remain professionally competent and also able to take care of his health?

- What are Joe's fears about failing as a parent, husband, and caregiver? What can he and his wife do to ease those fears?

- Might it be possible and appropriate for the kids to become more involved in the lives of their grandparents?

- What are some of the resources available to help adult children manage "sandwich generation" responsibilities?

- Are we really thinking through long-term planning and getting all the resources available for caregiving?

Joe and his wife need to talk as partners, as members of the same team. Together they can begin to restructure their routine and their responsibilities so that Joe stays healthy and accepts that he doesn't have to be a superhero. There are many shifts they can make quickly that will ease this burden. For example, they can seek professional advice, hire a caregiver, and schedule regular dates and quiet time for the two of them alone. They can also schedule family time, which should include exercise and other activities that involve paying attention to one another. The family will be best served by this kind of preemptive planning. More family time and a greater division of responsibilities will result in less stress and a healthier Joe.

WHAT ABOUT YOU?

As you've seen, silent agreements can have great influence over whether you maintain your health or derail it. Do you put off advised health screenings because you silently decree that since you have no symptoms, there's nothing wrong with you? Do any diseases run in your family that you have put off being tested for? Maybe you haven't asked your new boyfriend to produce STI test results because you think that doing so would make for awkward conversation. What about that strange-looking mole? It's never exposed to the sun, and you can't see it easily, so maybe it's okay to just forget about it for now. Perhaps you've been feeling a little off for a long time but fear that telling someone might stigmatize you as mentally unsound; you've silently agreed that you don't need therapy because after all, you're not crazy, so why give anyone in your life reason to wonder about your mental state?

Do any of these scenarios sound familiar? They're very common silent agreements relative to our own health, born of fear, hopelessness, and aversion to discomfort. We tell ourselves that it's just more pleasant not to know because we are afraid. When our beliefs are tied to issues of strength or weakness, competence or incompetence, vitality or listlessness, we can find ourselves making silent agreements that limit the possibilities for our best possible wellness. These are beliefs worth challenging. This is why silent agreements about health are perhaps the most important to unearth, and the sooner the better.

CHAPTER 9

YOUR SILENT AGREEMENTS TOOL KIT

In our work with people of varied backgrounds and histories, we've observed that when people improve one relationship in their lives, that change leads to improvement in other aspects of their lives. These people become stronger, happier, and healthier. Now that you've read earlier chapters and done some of the exercises, you may be aware of some silent agreements of your own. The exercises in this chapter will help you further explore your own silent agreements and demonstrate the dramatic changes you can achieve if you're willing to speak up for yourself and unearth the silent agreements in your life.

The following section offers a more complete tool to determine if you in fact have a silent agreement. Then it will help you uncover the beliefs, assumptions, and expectations that lie beneath it and ultimately enable you to dissect those core issues. The exercise can be found in its entirety at the back of the book.

HOW DO I KNOW I HAVE A SILENT AGREEMENT?

Exploring and Communicating Your Assumptions, Beliefs, and Expectations

Consider a situation in which you think you might be part of a silent agreement, perhaps with a partner, child, parent, friend, or colleague. Then complete the following sentence starters to understand more.

- I grew up with the belief that (focus on a belief that relates to the situation) . . .

- I assumed that he/she/they knew that . . .

- I therefore expected that he/she/they would . . .

- I told (did not tell) him/her/them what I believe about . . .

- I told (did not tell) him/her/them what I assumed he/she/they knew . . .

- I told (did not tell) him/her/them that I expected . . .

HOW TO DO IT

Agreement Example
You and your partner keep having the same argument. You're ready to move in together, and your partner thinks it's too soon. You can't come up with a solution, but neither

one of you is willing to suggest that you part ways. If you do this exercise, your thoughts might sound something like the *italicized sentence completions below:*

YOU:

> **I grew up with the belief that** *if someone loves me, he or she will make a clear commitment to me.*

> **I assumed that you knew that** *if you can't commit to your loved one's wishes, you're indicating that you don't really love him.*

> **I therefore expected that** *because we're in love, you would want us to live together to show your love for me, your commitment to our relationship, and your intention to marry me.*

Note Your Communication
Now check in with yourself about how well you've communicated your expectations and select the choice that applies best to you.

For example:

I told my partner that I believe that if he loves me, he needs to make a stronger commitment.

I SAID THAT   I DIDN'T SAY THAT   I'M NOT READY YET

I told my partner that I assumed he knew that to me moving in together demonstrates his love AND his level of commitment.

I SAID THAT   I DIDN'T SAY THAT   I'M NOT READY YET

I told my partner that therefore I expect him to move in
with me to show that he ultimately plans to marry me.

I SAID THAT   I DIDN'T SAY THAT   I'M NOT READY YET

Identify Your Obstacles
This exercise will help you identify obstacles to communicating your expectations.

On a scale of 1 to 10, how closely does his/her behavior
match my expectations? (1 = doesn't match at all, 10 = the
closest possible match) Circle your response.

1   2   3   4   5   6   7   8   9   10

Then answer yes or no to the following questions. If you
are not sure how to answer these questions, you might
want to consider how ready you are to communicate your
expectations.

- If my expectations are not being met, am I waiting
  for him/her to change?

- Am *I* waiting for the other person to talk to me
  about an issue that is critical to our relationship?

- Would I like to bring it up myself but feel stuck
  because of fear or my aversion to confrontation?

- How long have I been waiting? Why? What fears
  do I have about communicating my expectations?

HOW TO DO IT

Example

OBSTACLES YOU NOTED:

In doing this exercise, **you're likely very conscious that it's now a year that you've been waiting** for him to start looking for a place to share, and that you **want him to start talking** to you more about why he hasn't moved forward on this. **Do your expectations of each other match?** Maybe you can also admit to yourself that although your partner loves you, you're afraid that **he doesn't love you enough to want to move in with you or marry you** and that maybe no one else will.

FEATURES OF MY SILENT AGREEMENTS

Next, check all the statements below that apply to your situation.

When you do these exercises, don't be rattled if more than one or two of these situations apply to you. Silent agreements tend to have layers, so they can show up in many ways.

- You have values that you haven't talked about.

- Your expectations are not being met.

- You're waiting for the other party to change what he or she expects.

- You're waiting for the other party to talk about an issue that's related to your expectations and that is critical for the well-being of the relationship.

- You have fears that encourage your silence, and/or you value aspects of your relationship that encourage your silence.

- You have only recently realized that this has been going on in your relationship.

If you have run into difficulty completing these exercises, you may need to explore your agreements with yourself.

Now that you've seen the examples, try to complete all the exercises in each section to find out if you have a silent agreement.

You can begin by thinking about a situation in which you think there may be a silent agreement in place. It may be showing up in the arguments you have with your intimate partner, in your frustrations with your work and career, or in the burdens you feel with family and friends. Find a quiet place without distractions and give yourself the time to answer each question thoughtfully. You may need to complete the questions over a period of time.

Remember:

- Take your time and work through the questions in all sections honestly.

- It's important to think about your core beliefs and assumptions.

- Give a lot of thought to the beliefs that were in place before your current relationship issue arose.

- If you reflect upon and complete the exercises with care, you should be able to figure out whether you're engaged in silent agreements.

A NEW APPROACH TO COMMUNICATION

When you have completed the exercises above and are ready to share, consider the following:

- Which part of this situation would you like to talk about if you could?

- After exploring these issues, how might you think differently about the situation?

- Describe how you typically communicate a sensitive topic to someone important to you— your spouse or boss or family.

- What rules or guidelines can you now set up that will help you tell people the truth about your needs? Consider mood, context, timing, location. For example, you might make sure to talk when you're calm and well rested, set a time limit for the conversation, and write out your main points beforehand.

- Share your thoughts about your intention to communicate within guidelines safe for everyone. For example, "Can we talk this weekend, even if just a bit, about how much longer your brother will live here?"

Let's look again at our example to see how you might complete this part of the exercise and how it might help you to move forward.

HOW TO DO IT

Agreement Example

Which part of this issue would you like to talk about?
You might tell your partner that you interpret his unwillingness to move in with you to mean that he doesn't love you enough to marry you, but that for you, your moving in together will solidify your belief in his love and commitment.

How can you think differently?
At this point you need to know if he truly wants the relationship. The real roots of the silent agreement are your fear that you'll lose your partner and his fear that he may feel incompetent in a permanent relationship if he's not successful enough before making a firm commitment. Try to explore the fears behind his resistance and your insecurities. The goal is to find a way to strengthen your commitment to each other that both of you can be comfortable with.

How do you typically communicate about a sensitive topic?
Maybe you realize that you're inclined to complain when your partner doesn't fully engage in the conversation. This time tell your partner what you'd like him to think about over the next week, so he'll be prepared to have a positive and constructive conversation.

What guidelines can you set up that will help make the conversation go well?

Because you know that your partner is working long, hard days, you'll ask him when he can spend some uninterrupted time with you when he's rested. If you both come to the conversation well rested and calm, you'll be able to think clearly and will be more optimistic. If you know that one of you can tolerate long conversations better than the other, start with five to ten minutes and plan to revisit the subject another time if either of you runs out of steam.

Have the Conversation

The final step in this exercise is to have the conversation you've been preparing for. Share what you have believed, assumed, and expected about the situation. Talk about what you now understand has been going on because of those beliefs, assumptions, and expectations. Invite the other party to do the same. This should help both of you to see how you each have participated in the silent agreement.

HOW TO DO IT

Agreement Example

What you might say to your partner:

> **I believed that** if you love me **you would want to make a commitment to me** at this point in our relationship. **I assumed you knew that the next step** in our relationship would be one that **will show** our commitment to each other and lead us to **our ultimate**

goal of getting married. Because you've told me how much you love me, and we've been together for two years, I **expected you to** want to make this **move with me**. The fact that you have resisted moving in together makes me wonder if you truly want to be with me. **I have silently agreed to stay in the relationship** as it is because **I'm afraid to find out that you may not love me enough** to marry me in the end. **I hope we can talk more about** what our underlying fears are. We might find that they're not even related to this issue. Is that okay?

Options and Consequences

Remember that there is no one way to address a silent agreement. You may decide that the agreement works for you and doesn't need to be changed. You might decide that there are only some elements of your silent agreement that need your attention. Or you might decide to reject the whole agreement because you don't like it, need it, or find it helpful. The choice is always yours, but as you've seen, there are consequences to the choices you make.

As you explore the silent agreements in your relationships, it's helpful for you to consider what you might want to do in each of the three scenarios we've identified throughout the book: keep it, reframe it, or eliminate it. The grid that follows offers a look at possible outcomes of the different choices. Use the grid to help you decide what to do about the silent agreements you've uncovered.

Think about a silent agreement that exists in one of your relationships. Write the silent agreement in the first column. Then consider the possible outcomes of the options you have for handling it.

MY SILENT AGREEMENT	SILENT AGREEMENT OPTIONS	SILENT AGREEMENT IMPACT
	Keep it. They match; they work.	They provide contentment.
	Keep it. They don't match; they don't work.	You keep suffering, you live with it.
	Eliminate it. They don't match; they don't work. They hurt and/or disappoint.	You feel relief; change seems possible, easier.
	Reframe it. You have new insights; you are willing to adjust.	You build on mutual understanding and develop shared goals.

Key Questions for the Grid

Is there any action that will realistically change or modify your situation?

Can you live with the outcome?

Will you be satisfied with the outcome?

SILENT AGREEMENTS WITH YOURSELF

Remember: Silent agreements with others begin with the ones you have with yourself. If you've had difficulty answering our questions about silent agreements in your relationships, it might be time to explore your silent agreements with yourself. Following is a preliminary checklist of feelings and thoughts to help you see if a silent agreement you have with yourself is at work.

Have you experienced this before?

Been silent about your pain, your tension, or promises you've made to yourself?

Found yourself making decisions that don't line up with your values?

Experienced a conflict that keeps repeating itself?

Engaged in behavior that contradicts an essential belief or value of yours?

Find that you are no longer content to hide your feelings or expectations?

Find that you're uncomfortable with silence during difficult conversations?

Saying yes to any of these may indicate that you're ready to start asking yourself direct questions to unpack a silent agreement you have with yourself.

Changing Your Agreements with Yourself

Change often involves choice and commitment. Making the choice to explore your silent agreements with yourself is the first step. Now make the commitment. Only you will know when you're ready for this very personal exploration. You might ask yourself:

- Can I live with what I might discover, even if it's not what I expect?

- Once I uncover my silent agreements with myself, will I have the capacity to change them?

- Is it even necessary to determine why I've kept silent?

- Has my silence benefited me, cost me, or both?

When you're able to recognize what's beneath your repeated cycle of avoiding, ignoring, or postponing self-awareness, you're ready to have honest self-talk. Try to identify the ways the silent agreement serves to sustain a dysfunctional situation. If your agreements are going well and are easy to live by (e.g., "I will never lie to my husband"), then great! That's because the functional agreement, though silent, is supporting what you value, believe, or assume. But if circumstances shift because of a life-changing event such as divorce, death, or a serious illness, or for no apparent reason, a silent agreement ("I will never let my spouse know exactly how much money I make" or "I'll never admit how terrified I am of dying") can surface and cause conflict. In cases like these, try to establish when and why you created this silent agreement.

- Do you think you might be able to consider your silent agreement from another person's point of view? An objective friend (who isn't part of the agreement) might be able to offer a helpful perspective.

- What memories do you have that will help you understand what's behind your silent agreement with yourself?

Uncovering Silent Agreements with Yourself

Exploring your agreements with yourself requires you to use insight and self-examination to lift the silence and prepare the way for a new agreement, one that's more in line with your needs and goals. When you're ready to start, remember to use our general guidelines for uncovering silent agreements.

1. Look back at your past.
This step is critical, one that you cannot skip. When exploring your silent agreements with yourself, try to think back to the origins of why you say and do certain things, and why in this

case you've remained silent. *Why?* Consider how earlier interactions with your family and friends have played a role in shaping your behaviors and current feelings about yourself. Developing this kind of self-awareness will help you understand and articulate current silent agreements and put you in control of those that may come to pass in the future.

2. Spend some quiet time with your thoughts. Recognize the path that got you here.

Whether you're trying to work through a silent agreement in a personal relationship or one in your professional life, consider options for where and when you can spend uninterrupted time focusing on this process.

3. Discern what is important.

Do your best to leave judgment and blame behind. Acknowledge the emotion but focus on what you want to achieve. When you take responsibility for your actions rather than blaming or accusing yourself, positive things can happen. The goal is to work through your thoughts, feelings, and beliefs to achieve a new understanding. And remember, insisting that things continue to go your way is *not always* your best resolution.

4. Be courageous.

Take a deep breath and say aloud what your agreement with yourself has kept silent. By break-

ing the silence, you're helping to eliminate negative emotions like guilt and fear. People who take
these first steps usually emerge feeling proud,
courageous, and even lighter.

**5. Move from reactive to proactive. Understand-
ing your silent agreement with yourself will help
you relate to the important people in your life.**
When you move from being reactive to being
proactive about your well-being, you commit to a
form of staying awake at the wheel. This includes
not letting a lot of time pass without checking in
with yourself about new or residual silent agreements and making sure that you're appreciating
yourself and feeling valued in your relationships.

As you proactively seek to explore your silent
agreements with others, develop new ways to
open a dialogue. Avoid phrases like "We'll never
see eye to eye" in favor of phrases like "I want to
listen more and try to understand why you so
passionately believe as you do." Employing this
kind of language will come more naturally with
practice and will deliver great results.

We can't overstate the importance of making a practice of examining the underlying
triggers—your beliefs, assumptions, values, and
expectations—that lead you to create silent agreements in the first place. This kind of exploration
will give you greater control over your part in
creating and discussing silent agreements.

*Still Struggling to Start the Conversation
with Yourself or Someone Else?*

You may need help to move forward. Pushing beyond the
silence sounds easy enough, but if you have emotional
baggage of any size, this process can require strength
and support. You'll have to work to overcome the fears
that stand in your way—fear of confrontation, fear of disappointment, fear of disappointing another, fear of losing a relationship, and fear of failure, to name only a few.
Finding reliable information and resources and engaging
a caring and well-trained therapist or coach may help increase your self-esteem and enable you to practice having
difficult conversations. A simple willingness to revise your
approach is a very powerful tool, so take a deep breath and
trust the process.

FINDING YOUR OWN WAY

Try to consider your silent agreements without internalizing negative feelings. This practice will help you to move
from reacting negatively to proactively deciding where to
focus your attention.

Throughout this process, remember to:

- Calmly remind yourself that it's human to
  sometimes send mixed signals. You're not alone
  in doing this.

- Reassure yourself that with patience and
  understanding you can explore different ways
  of addressing your agreements that may deliver
  better results.

- Consider talking to someone you trust to hear you out—no advice, just listening. Don't be surprised if that person opens up to you about *his or her* silent agreements.

- Recognize that facing difficult truths can lead to greater fulfillment.

- Look for those things that inspire you.

BREAKING THE SILENCE

After you emerge from the emotional desert of silence, be aware that an outpouring of unrealized needs, fantasies, fears, wishes, and heightened expectations may overwhelm both you and the other party at first. Summoning the courage to stretch the limits of your relationship with another and with yourself will make you feel stronger and more alive.

As you push through and past your silent agreements, you may find yourself wanting to question yourself and others directly to better understand what drives you and your relationships. Practice communicating with honesty and openness and ask pointed questions without apology. While not everyone will be as verbal as you are, don't shy away from asking for straight answers. You'll find that conversations that used to be awkward will become easier, and this kind of open communication helps *prevent* the formation of silent agreements.

Good News About Breaking Silent Agreements
This task is not always easy and won't be mastered overnight. It takes practice and a willingness to strip the subject down to its most basic truths. Children do this naturally until we teach them to be politer. The good news is that deep down, you have an inkling of what's really going on. After you bring it to the surface, you'll feel lighter.

Dos and Don'ts
Keep these dos and don'ts in mind as you work on addressing your silent agreements. They will help you to stay the course with energy and optimism.

BEFORE: PREPARING TO ADDRESS YOUR SILENT AGREEMENTS

Do participate in uplifting rituals like sports, running, prayer, meditation, working out, yoga, massages, or hanging out with friends. This will set you on the right path for the work you're about to do.

Do envision positive outcomes.

Do share with those you trust that you are embarking on this path and want their support.

Don't begin this process when you feel overwhelmed. You'll need all your resources during this journey.

Don't take on other emotional projects.

Don't engage in multitasking.

DURING: ONCE THE JOURNEY IS UNDER WAY

Do focus on your health.

Do challenge your self-defeating personal habits (excessive drinking, impulsive behavior, explosive anger, overreacting, etc.). Get professional help. Don't wait until the behavior is out of control.

Do take breaks. Make time to enjoy yourself and to do something you love. This helps you to keep things in perspective and to maintain your sparkle.

Do pace yourself. Rome wasn't built in a day (nor was any other city).

Don't forget to stay connected to friends and loved ones who may not realize you're going through emotional upheaval. Allow yourself to spend time with those who seem most helpful. Give yourself permission to spend time however you deem best for you.

Don't think and talk about silent agreements all of the time. You'll exhaust your emotional resources.

Don't be hard on yourself if the going gets difficult. The difficulty is to be expected and means you're working hard.

AFTER: THE BEAT GOES ON

Do praise yourself for a job well done.

Do revisit your new agreements to make sure they're working for you.

Do continue open, candid communication with others.

Don't think the job is finished. This is an ongoing process that can be both rewarding and fun.

Don't expect silent agreements to be gone forever. They have a way of popping up, but now you have the tools to address them.

Don't lose patience with new relationships. Give others time to warm to this approach, to take an honest look at themselves, and then to trust you enough to share.

Reconstructing Silent Agreements

Once you identify the silent agreements that operate within your relationships, you'll be equipped to reconstruct, eliminate, or accept them. You'll be able to see that two people really are co-owners of silent agreements that they share. Together, you can choose to keep the parts of the agreement that make sense, discard the parts that don't, or simply start from scratch with a new understanding that meets the needs that have now been shared openly. The very act of releasing yourself and your relationships from the silent agreements that hinder you is enriching. Now you can step out of the roles you've been playing and simply be who you are.

Q & A

Q: *What if my partner and I were to go to premarital counseling to spot our agreements and prevent relationship problems down the line?*
A: Unless the silent agreements operating inside you and in your relationships are patently obvious, which is rarely the case, premarital counseling may not enable you and your partner to anticipate how you will handle all the issues you'll have to face during the life of your relationship. Significant life events can trigger unhealthy responses from silent agreements made in the past; these can't always be predicted. However, premarital counseling can assist you in becoming aware of your silent agreements and in learning to openly communicate about them, and that can help your marriage tremendously.

Q: *Will I now have to discuss every thought and feeling that enters my head in order to avoid creating a silent agreement with my friend, spouse, coworker, or sibling?*
A: Of course that's impossible. Keep in mind that we all live with silent agreements whether or not we consciously created them. Rather than expressing all your thoughts aloud, spend time trying to understand issues in their early stages if you can. After you've given yourself a chance to observe and marshal your thoughts about a situation, you'll then be in a better position to productively share them with the other people involved.

Q: *Don't we all have silent agreements with others and ourselves?*
A: Yes, we all do. Many of them we simply live with until we decide we want to change and to develop the courage to openly discuss what we're feeling internally.

Q: *Why are silences so important to us?*
A: Silent feelings and thoughts forced underground keep us feeling safe. Even though they lead to behaviors that can work against the very outcomes we want, we may still prefer to avoid the risk of full disclosure.

Q: *How are we able to be in intimate relationships with all of those feelings and thoughts we find unacceptable?*
A: People often choose partners who also have secretly stored feelings, beliefs, and expectations as well as ways of hiding them. Both of you may invest a lot of energy in keeping your silences and "agreeing" that hiding out from "unacceptable" feelings is the least risky way to interact with each other. Because we often find others who appear to be perfect candidates to share our silent agreements, we're able to remain in these relationships for a long time. When one or both of you feel the need to break or change the agreement, you're likely to have difficulty maintaining the relationship in its current state.

Q: *Why don't we just ask the essential questions of our partners, family members, coworkers, and friends early? Why not find out the truth to begin with?*
A: Silent agreements offer protection from our having to disclose what might be difficult to hear, see, feel, or

know about each other or ourselves. We passively agree to ignore the other's issues so that he or she will do us the favor of being quiet about ours. It's a kind of "don't ask, don't tell" connection that we keep making with others, primarily because it's the type of agreement we have with ourselves.

Q: *Do folks ever come up with silent agreements that are helpful to their relationships?*
A: Yes, they absolutely do. And we often don't notice such agreements because they complement healthy needs. For example, say your husband likes his coffee piping hot in the morning. He's also slow to wake up and get going. You, on the other hand, are a peppy, take-charge woman, an early riser who likes to get up and get out the door. One day, when he's just getting into the shower, you tell him to whistle when he's ready for his coffee. He does, and you bring it up to him while he's still getting ready for the day. Then off you dash to work. You two continue this tradition for the next forty years. He gets to take his time without being pressured, and you get to perform a small gesture that speeds things up and makes you both feel good. It's a lovely example of a silent agreement that goes unnoticed because it works so well for both people.

Q: *What about as we get older? Should we still do all of this digging for our silent agreements? After all, if it ain't broke, why fix it?*
A: As we all know, people in long-standing relationships aren't necessarily happy couples. Yes, some figure out a way to coexist with a minimum of obvious

tension or discord. Nevertheless, the silent agreements can strangle the joy out of a relationship at a time of life when a couple may have more time and fewer responsibilities. So instead of having the time of their lives, they're often stuck in a rut wondering, "Is that all there is?" So yes, anyone at any stage of a relationship can benefit from holding an agreement up to the light. People can keep what's healthy and works for them. If they work through some old and not-so-healthy silent agreements and learn to express what's behind them, their golden years can be truly golden.

Q: *What about my sex life? Can I expect to have great sex if I have unresolved silent agreements?*

A: That depends on where you are in the silent agreement process. If you and your partner(s) have been trying to uncover your silent agreements, the effort to unclutter your relationship in this way will help you unclutter your bedroom encounters as well. So if you've been having good sex so far, discovering and adjusting your silent agreements might lead to your enjoying an even more powerful, connected, spiritual, or exciting sex life. On the other hand, if great sex is the foundation of your silent agreement, you could go on reveling in the sex until one or both of you have the need to uncover what's being masked by the "great sex agreement." You won't necessarily stop enjoying sex once you uncover the hidden agreement, but you might begin to realize that there are other satisfying aspects of the relationship that will also sustain it.

Tips

- When you begin this work in your relationships, be prepared for resistance from others. This is new and somewhat threatening stuff at first. Be ready to be told that you're "making a mountain out of a molehill," are "too sensitive," or are "trying to create problems where there are none." Consider this resistance to be a sign that you're on the right path.

- If you notice that in most of your relationships you begin changing into someone who seeks the approval of others or who often ignores your own values, this is a sign that a silent agreement may exist. In this type of relationship, you rarely feel that you're being yourself. The exercises will help you uncover this pattern.

- If you're beginning to suspect that you're constantly choosing relationships with controlling people, you may have a silent agreement with yourself that perpetuates this pattern. The controlling person may be a mate, a boss, a spouse, or a sibling, and the form of control may be active or passive; the common element is that you are choosing a dependent role in the relationship. For example, are you always selecting a partner or friends who are emotionally unavailable or immature? He or she may be passively controlling you by keeping you in limbo, on edge, or confused about where you stand. You may be agreeing to this kind of control and avoiding conversation about it because it is *less scary for you than being alone*. This is a common belief in some silent agreements.

- If you're the one who becomes the reliable caretaker in most of your relationships, you may be in a provider/protector agreement. The key is to look at your patterns, which are clues to the feelings underneath the silent agreements you make. If you feel ignored, undervalued, overworked, overwhelmed, or more connected to the lives you protect than to your own, it's likely you've been involved in a caregiving silent agreement that does not take you into account.

- In the sexual arena, don't ignore your feelings, whatever they may be. This area is often a landmine of silent agreements, with each party tiptoeing to avoid disaster. When you find the courage, work to uncover an agreement between you and your partner; you can develop a positive sense of yourself and that will allow you more pleasure!

APPENDIX

If you want to focus primarily on the exercises found in the book, we have compiled them on the next few pages. Here is a list.

I. A SILENT AGREEMENT APPROACH TO COMMUNICATION

Begin by thinking about a situation in which you think there may be a silent agreement in place. It may be showing up in the arguments you have with your intimate partner, in your frustrations with your work and career, or in the burdens you feel your family and friends have laid on you. Find a quiet place and give yourself the time to answer the following questions thoughtfully without distractions. You may need to complete them a little at a time.
Remember:

- Take your time and work through the questions honestly.

- Think about your core values, principles, beliefs, and assumptions.

- Give a lot of thought to the beliefs that were in place before your current relationship issue arose.

- If this exercise is done with care, after you reflect upon and complete it, you should achieve some clarity about whether you're engaged in silent agreements.

- Consider mood, context, timing, and location.

- Share your thoughts about your intention to communicate within guidelines safe for everyone. For example, "Can we talk this weekend, even if just a bit, about how much longer your brother will live here?"

II. WAYS OF COMMUNICATING

The following reflective questions can help direct your conversations:

- Which part of this situation would you like to talk about if you could?

- After exploring these issues, how might you think differently about the situation?

- Describe how you typically communicate a sensitive topic to your spouse/boss/family, etc.

- What rules or guidelines can you now set up that will help you tell people the truth about your needs? For example, you might make sure to talk when you're calm and well rested, set a time limit for the conversation, and write out your main points beforehand.

Conversation Starters

You can begin by letting your boss, friend, family member, or lover know that you want to try a new way of communicating to address what is going on between you. Here are some examples of how you might communicate your concerns.

- You and I share a problem. We've both let this linger. I hope we can work through this together.

- Things have fallen apart between us. In the meantime, just know how much I love (trust, respect, care about) you. I don't want us to act as if our problem doesn't exist.

- I need a weekend away, a time-out to get myself together so I can focus on forgiveness and how we can talk through this without guilt or shame.

- I'm concerned that there are issues we haven't talked about that are affecting how we work together. I wonder if you have concerns about this, too.

- Talking about this is difficult for me, but I'm hoping we can help each other say what we need to say.

Conversation Responses

These are phrases, statements, questions, and comments that may come up in response to conversation starters.

- I haven't been fully open with you either.

- I would like to open up more, but it is too painful right now.

- It seems to me this is a part of a larger conversation.

- This feels like the continuation of a conversation we had a long time ago. I thought we settled it.

- I need to think about this a few more days. I will let you know when I am ready to talk about it.

- I am not sure you want to know how I *really* feel. If you do, you will need to listen without interrupting me. Is that something you can do when you are ready?

- Why discuss what is already working out fine for us? Why talk about it?

- I've been keeping silent too long. I guess I thought talking about it would make it worse.

- I am not ready to think about this now. Give me twenty minutes after tonight's game is over, okay?

III. EXPLORING AND COMMUNICATING ASSUMPTIONS, BELIEFS, AND EXPECTATIONS

Consider a situation in which you think you might be part of a silent agreement, perhaps with a partner, a child, a parent, a friend, or a colleague. Then complete the following sentence starters to understand more.

- I grew up with the belief that (focus on a belief that relates to the situation) . . .

- I assumed that he/she/they knew that . . .

- I therefore expected that he/she/they would . . .

- I told (did not tell) him/her/them what I believe about . . .

- I told (did not tell) him/her/them what I assumed he/she/they knew . . .

- I told (did not tell) him/her/them that I expected . . .

IV. NOTING YOUR COMMUNICATION/ IDENTIFYING YOUR OBSTACLES

This exercise will help you clarify how well you're communicating your expectations.

On a scale of 1 to 10, how closely does his/her behavior match my expectations? (1 = doesn't match at all; 10 = the closest possible match)

Circle your response.

1   2   3   4   5   6   7   8   9   10

Answer yes or no. If you can't answer yes or no, it's possible that you're not ready to communicate your expectations to the following questions:

- If my expectations are not being met, am I waiting for him/her to change?

- Am *I* waiting for the other person to talk to me about an issue that is critical to our relationship?

- Would I like to bring it up myself but feel stuck because of fear or my aversion to confrontation?

- How long have I been waiting? Why? What fears do I have about communicating my expectations?

V. CROSS SECTION OF BELIEFS, EXPECTATIONS, AND BEHAVIORS

Fill out the table below, noting your beliefs and expectations that apply to the situation you are considering. At the same time, include a description of your behavior so you can see how well it matches (or not) with your beliefs and expectations. Also note your partner's behavior (or that of your family member, friend, coworker, or boss) to see if it matches your beliefs and expectations.

	MY BELIEFS	MY EXPECTATIONS
MY BEHAVIOR		
MY PARTNER'S BEHAVIOR		

VI. THE SILENT AGREEMENT GRID

The following grid offers a look at possible outcomes of different choices. Use it to help you decide what to do about the silent agreements you've uncovered. Think about a silent agreement that exists and consider the possible outcomes of the options you have for handling it.

MY SILENT AGREEMENT	SILENT AGREEMENT OPTIONS	SILENT AGREEMENT IMPACT
	Keep it. They match; they work.	They provide contentment.
	Keep it. They don't match; they don't work.	You keep suffering, you live with it.
	Eliminate it. They don't match; they don't work. They hurt and/or disappoint.	You feel relief; change seems possible, easier.
	Reframe it. You have new insights; you are willing to adjust.	You build on mutual understanding and develop shared goals.

Key Silent Agreement Grid Questions

- Is there any action that will realistically change or modify your situation?

- Can you live with the impact and outcome?

- Will you be satisfied with the outcome?

ACKNOWLEDGMENTS

As authors, educators, therapists, and consultants, we have seen countless individuals, couples, and families searching for more fulfillment in their personal and work lives.

This book has given us the opportunity to dream and bring forth the hopes and aspirations of others to make meaningful choices for more fulfilling relationships at home, work, and play.

Special gratitude goes to all of those directly involved with our book:

- Harmony/Rodale for the production of our book and Michele Eniclerico, our editor, for her expertise and time in making Silent Agreements™ come alive.

- Regina Brooks, our agent and owner of Serendipity Literary Agency, for her patience, direction, and expertise in shaping and negotiating our contract, finding key collaborators along the way, and helping to shape our proposal. Regina, thank you for teaching us the ropes and pushing us through to this moment. You are our agent par excellence!

- Jodi Fodor for her patience as our developmental editor. You're a true team player; thank you for helping us find a common voice to reach our readers. You are really talented and fun to work with. We also thank Jean Staeheli, Virginia La Plante, Anita Diggs, Joan Lester, Diane Patrick, and Ruth Mills for their skillful editorial support.

- Anna Ghosh, Elaine Brown, and Hara Marano for their great-hearted offering of clarity and insight in the early stages.

- Our mentors and book coaches, Susan Jones Johnson, Esq., and Sheryl Hilliard Tucker, who provided invaluable advice and guidance and contributed to the organization and flow of the manuscript; and Marie Brown, who provided deeply appreciated support and uplifted our voice in the process.

- Raoul Davis, Merilee Kern, and Paula Moreno for helping us to build our platform, craft and provide visual voice to our message, and synthesize our brand. Thank you for the stellar publicity and marketing you provided.

- Ellis Echevarria for his design support.

- Jocquelle Caiby for her assistance with forming and clarifying our proposal.

The authors can be reached at www.SilentAgreements.com.

REFERENCES

INTRODUCTION: WHAT SILENT AGREEMENTS ARE
AND HOW THEY AFFECT OUR RELATIONSHIPS

1. D. W. Winnicott, "Ego Distortion in Terms of True and False Self." *The Maturational Processes and the Facilitating Environment: Studies in the Theory of Emotional Development.* New York: International Universities Press, 1965, 140–52.

2. Murray Bowen, *Family Therapy in Clinical Practice.* Northvale, NJ: Jason Aronson, 1985.

3. Robert Kegan, *The Evolving Self: Problem and Process in Human Development.* Cambridge, MA: Harvard University Press, 1982.

INDEX

254   Index

ABOUT THE AUTHORS

Dr. Linda D. Anderson is a clinical psychologist, life coach, and therapist. Having a long history of inspiring success in others, Dr. Anderson currently teaches, consults, and empowers in a manner embraced by a diverse range of individuals and organizations. She is a professor at Hostos Community College, City University of New York, and a consulting psychologist at the Dalton School. Driven to achieve results with flexibility and a cooperative spirit, she possesses a unique ability to engage and inspire others. Her research investigating women's perceptions of power and their vulnerability to coerced sexual experiences has led her to teach, write, and counsel others from a perspective of critical compassion and empowerment.

Dr. Anderson graduated from Boston University with a double major in Spanish language/literature and psychology, and earned her doctorate in clinical psychology at Columbia University. She has served as staff psychologist in the Department of Child and Adolescent Psychiatry at

Beth Israel Medical Center and has taught at Teachers College, Columbia University, and at Bard College at Simon's Rock. She writes about topics that explore the psychology of success and cultural diversity, silent agreements at the workplace, challenges facing women, and work/life balance, as well as achieving critical compassion in the classroom. She has appeared in popular media and television outlets.

Dr. Sonia R. Banks is a results-driven clinical psychologist and behavioral health strategist who makes the most of transitions we all go through when reaching our desired goals. Dr. Banks uses behavioral play to change attitudes and introduce people to their "possible selves." Whether she's training, lecturing, interviewing, or facilitating, Dr. Banks brings her full self to the experience and invites you to join her on the journey to self-discovery, awareness, and love. Dr. Banks has a doctorate and master's degree in Clinical Psychology from George Washington University, and a Master of Arts degree in Human Resource Management from the New School for Social Research. She received a Bachelor of Arts degree in Psychology from Wellesley College. She has a proven record of designing for authentic personal power as easily as for qualitative research-based behavioral interventions. Dr. Banks has counseled and coached hundreds of people using her trailblazing cross-disciplinary approach to relationship consulting. She has been a featured therapist in several articles published in *Essence* magazine and contributed to articles for the *American Journal of Public Health*. She is a diagnostic psychotherapist for several relationship conflicts on network shows, has been quoted in local newspapers, and has appeared several times on NBC, on ABC, and on Cox Radio. She currently leads a passionate process to improve quality of life, and through @Play infuses playful activities as a tool for consulting, coaching, and team engagement, inspiring everyone from executives and entrepreneurs to couples and families.

Dr. Michele L. Owens is a clinical psychologist and psychotherapist known for her ability to support while challenging, to inspire while facilitating, and to foster and enhance personal growth. She is passionate about relationship development in women, couples, and families, and is dedicated to improving mental health in adolescents and young adults. Toward that end she has conducted workshops on improving communication, unearthing silent agreements, and developing sustainable, healthy relationships. She has also treated countless adolescents and developed programs to help them and their families navigate this critical time in the life cycle. Dr. Owens has a unique perspective on the ways in which culture and tradition can support and strengthen mental health and wellness and has created integrated programs for that purpose. In addition, she has designed and conducted workshops on diversity and multicultural competence.

Dr. Owens earned her undergraduate degree in sociology and psychology at Case Western Reserve University. She is a graduate of the Derner Institute of Advanced Psychological Studies at Adelphi University, where she earned her PhD. Dr. Owens has lent her clinical expertise to several colleges and institutions, including Columbia

University, City College of New York, Hofstra University, and the Einstein College of Medicine. She has appeared in multiple media outlets, and her writings can be found in the award-winning book *Psychotherapy with African American Women* and in *The Psychology of Black Boys and Adolescents*. Dr. Owens has a private practice in New York City, mentors budding clinicians, and is the senior psychologist at Prep for Prep, a premier academic and leadership development organization for underserved adolescents.